Other Works by Dana Adam Shapiro

BOOKS

The Every Boy: A Novel

MOVIES

Murderball

Monogamy

You Can Be RIGHT
(or You Can Be MARRIED)

Looking for Love in the Age of Divorce

DANA ADAM SHAPIRO

SCRIBNER

New York London Toronto Sydney New Delhi

SCRIBNER
A Division of Simon & Schuster, Inc.
1230 Avenue of the Americas
New York, NY 10020

First Scribner hardcover edition September 2012

SCRIBNER and design are registered trademarks of The Gale Group, Inc., used under license by Simon & Schuster, Inc., the publisher of this work.

For information about special discounts for bulk purchases, please contact Simon & Schuster Special Sales at 1-866-506-1949 or business@simonandschuster.com.

The Simon & Schuster Speakers Bureau can bring authors to your live event. For more information or to book an event contact the Simon & Schuster Speakers Bureau at 1-866-248-3049 or visit our website at www.simonspeakers.com.

Manufactured in the United States of America

1   3   5   7   9   10   8   6   4   2

ISBN 978-1-4516-5777-7
ISBN 978-1-4516-5779-1 (ebook)

For Rachel, my big sister

It ought to make us feel ashamed when we talk like we know
what we're talking about when we talk about love.

—RAYMOND CARVER

Cowardice and courage
are never without a measure of affectation.
Nor is love. Feelings are never true.
They play with their mirrors.

—JEAN BAUDRILLARD

My wife is out of town. I don't want to cheat on her outright
but I would love to find someone to play around with.
Maybe watch a porno or read an erotic story together,
massage, strip tease, lingerie modeling, take some pictures
with your camera, mutual masturbation, any other ideas?

—from the Casual Encounters listings on Craigslist

CONTENTS

You Can Be RIGHT
(or You Can Be MARRIED)

INTRODUCTION

My grandma keeps company with spirits. A Dewar's on the rocks every day at four o'clock on the button, and the spectral kind that rattle around her head. This isn't some crackpot theory; it's a matter of fact. They're here, now, passing through the walls of her old house on Cape Cod, where I've come to work on this book. For a long time, I thought it was a book about divorce: a bedside companion for the *boo-hoo* crowd, *Chicken Soup for Shattered Souls*. But while I may have set out to interview people about their most brutal breakups, I'm realizing now, almost four years in, that like most marital spats, *it's never about what it's about*.

It wasn't always like this—Grandma's spirits, I mean—only since my grandpa died, sixteen years ago, a few months shy of their fiftieth wedding anniversary. We talk about it often, this great love of hers, and as we do she sips her scotch, his drink, on her side of their bed. Still, always, on her side of their bed.

"To my Howard!" she says, toasting the ghost with his tumbler.

That's what she calls him now, *my Howard,* sometimes right to his face. It's a much younger face than I remember, black and white and framed on their bedroom wall. Back when he was here, in color, she always called him "Daddy."

To hear her tell it, she never had eyes for another. It was *b'shert,* she says—the Yiddish word for "destiny." They were neighborhood kids from the same side of the tracks of Haverhill, Massachusetts, a factory town that was known back then as Queen Slipper City because local workers manufactured almost 10 percent of the shoes worn in the United States. But the Cinderella

1

subtext wasn't lost on my grandma Rose, whose name no doubt influenced the tint of her gaze.

The first of eight children born to Russian immigrants in 1915, her head has been bumping up against the clouds ever since she could crawl. Where others saw dust, she found glitter, and she came of age air-trumpeting to Cole Porter, daydreaming of a trip to the moon on gossamer wings. And sure enough, as if her destiny had been written in calligraphy, she awoke one day in her teens to find that the love of her life was living just down the road.

My Howard.

"I got a car when I was sixteen years old, it was a convertible," she tells me. "And for my first ride, I went out looking for him. I wanted to show off a little. He was always very standoffish when it came to me but I used to run after him a little bit, I really did. So I put on my hat, and I looked very nice, and I drove by this place where all the boys used to hang around. And sure enough, there he was. I knew he'd be there. And I asked him: 'Would you like to go for a ride with me?' And he said, 'No. I'm busy.' Just like that: *I'm busy.*

"Well, I went home and I was hysterical. And my mother said, 'Stop your crying—what's the matter with you? If he didn't want to go with you, *so what*? You think he's such a *bargain*?' And I said, 'Well, Mother, he's a bargain to me.'"

When my grandpa died, I went snooping through his dresser, looking for clues to his character, hoping to find that long-lost tchotchke that would reveal the secret longings of a man's soul. His rusty dog tag from the war that earned him a Purple Heart now hangs from a chain on my office wall. His trusty flask sits on my desk, filled with a ceremonial shot of Dewar's. And next to that, from underneath a cache of Russian letters, I dug up a glossy fossil dated 1994: a mint-condition Valentine's Day card that he must have picked up at the pharmacy late that February morning. In flowery metallic script it says:

Hearts speak when words cannot.

Inside, written in an old man's poststroke, shaky hand:

Even though we have a lot of differences, and our communication is probably as bad as it can be, you have always been my sweetheart, and I guess will always be.
Please don't be mad.
Love,
H

It was a through-the-looking-glass moment. It's not like I thought they were Mark Antony and Cleopatra, but "as bad as it can be"? Late one afternoon, about three fingers after four, I showed the card to my grandma. She stared at it for a moment before revealing: "He could be a very cold cucumber, your grandfather. Never showed much affection. But I didn't care. I was perfectly happy when he was near me. I just loved him. No matter who I met—and I met some very nice guys—he always came first in my mind. Still, to this day."

Asked why she never considered going on a date after he passed away, she glanced at his picture on the wall and said, "Quit lookin' at me like that." Then, to me, "He was my angel." Pressed a bit about the practicality of fairy-tale phrases like *happily ever after* and *'til death do us part,* she sipped her scotch and responded with uncharacteristic candor. "You think I was gonna go out and find myself another guy? What for? So he could fart in my bed?"

Such is the romanticism on which I've been raised—Rose-colored, to be sure, but aware of its own rouge. I'm thirty-eight, a decade older than the average groom, and fast approaching that age when bachelors go from seeming curious to seeming weird. I've been single for the past two years, the longest stretch by far since falling for Lisa Newman when I was sixteen. We dated for more than three years, and since then I've had four more three-year relationships (the last two women, I lived with). I've been a serial monogamist for more than two decades, but I've never been engaged, my love stories inevitably falling victim to the three-year thud, that grounding period when it becomes painfully obvious that the honeymoon phase won't make it to the honeymoon.

In response to allegations of commitment phobia I've always maintained that I'm romantic to a fault—an idealist—incapable of the "settling" part of settling down. Of course, that's a classic idealist's defense, and as Jung warns, "Every form of addiction is bad, no matter whether the narcotic be alcohol or morphine or idealism." H. L. Mencken (who once called marriage "the end of hope") goes even further: "It is not materialism that is the chief curse of the world, as pastors teach, but idealism. Men get into trouble by taking their visions and hallucinations too seriously."

It's been almost four years since I started crisscrossing the country with an old tape recorder in an effort to avoid such trouble—to confront my addictions, my visions, and my hallucinations. With an open mind and a backpack full of batteries and microcassette tapes, I talked with hundreds of people, mostly strangers, asking them the types of inappropriately personal questions that you would never ask your friends. At times I felt like an embedded reporter, chronicling the lost battles of the sexes, filing dispatches from the front yards.

Amy likened the interview process to "telling war stories. I mean, how *did* I do those things? It's just unimaginable. I had a major fucking meltdown."

John spoke of liberation. "Once you get separated, you move on to other relationships, and suddenly they're wonderful. I mean, I'm not going to show you pictures, but I could."

Tasha talked about her dishonorable conduct: "I know I sound like a total bitch. I really was just a selfish, immature asshole."

I can relate. I, too, have been a selfish, immature asshole—

work-obsessed, unappreciative, oversensitive, overcritical, prideful, withholding, defensive, and I've often attempted to appear taller by standing on ceremony. At some fundamental level, this project began as a self-help manual in the purest sense: I was trying to help myself. I wanted to know what was wrong with me, why all five of my three-year relationships had ended. I wanted to understand women. And so, inspired by the work of Studs Terkel and Alfred Kinsey—and taking to heart the oft-paraphrased line about learning more from failure than from success—I set out to live vicariously through the romantic tragedies of others, hoping to glean some wisdom from the wreckage and to ultimately become so fluent in such failure that I would be able to avoid it in my own love life.

The "lightbulb moment" to write a book on this topic occurred the night before Thanksgiving in 2008. I was back home in Boston, newly single, having just separated from the last of my long-term girlfriends. An old buddy and I met up at a bar and we started talking about women and breakups. I went first: *We were perfect on paper, but we didn't have that X factor. She was gorgeous, smart, and talented, but we weren't telepathic—at all. You need to be at least a little telepathic, don't you think?*

He offered a sly smile, ordered a round of tequila, and then let it slide that he was separating from his wife of three years. Apparently she'd been having an affair while popping fistfuls of prescription painkillers, both on his dime. His face was brave but there was no hiding the truth. He was devastated.

"You can't change a person's character—yours *or* theirs," he said with the clarity of a burn victim. "Behavior, sure, you can change behavior. But character, *never*. So whatever it is you don't like about the person, magnify it by a million 'cus it only gets worse. If you still love them after that—*marry* them. If not . . ." He shook his head, disappointed, more at himself than at her. "*What the fuck was I thinking?*"

It was the fourth divorce I'd heard about that month. I wanted to get into the nitty-gritty but instead we toasted to better days and glossed over the real issues. Later that night, as if living in a cautionary metaphor, I lay awake in my childhood room, too big for my bed. I stared at the blank ceiling that used to be stickered with hundreds of glow-in-the-dark stars. I kept picturing my exes, magnified by a million. They looked pretty good. Why did I push them away? Had I made the mistake of a lifetime—five times in a row? Or had I dodged five bullets?

Unable to answer, I went downstairs to the breakfast table and made a list of all the people I knew under forty who had gotten divorced. I came up with fourteen names. It was a little early for the seven-year itch: *What the fuck were all these people thinking?* I wanted to peek through keyholes, rummage through medicine cabinets, read through deleted e-mails—anything to find out what *really* goes on behind closed doors. The word "autopsy" comes from *autopsia,* ancient Greek for "to see for oneself." To that end, I set out in search of corpses. I was looking for evidence, for *proof.* I needed to see for myself:

Why does love die?

Of course, it's tricky to go around prying into people's private lives without seeming like some kind of pervert. Couples tend to put a Facebook face on their relationships, and you can't just walk up to someone and ask them to drop the pose and start sharing their deepest secrets.

Unless you're writing a book. Then you can pry all you want.

As is often the case, I knew very little about this subject going in. I've been a journalist, a novelist, and a filmmaker, but never a husband or a therapist. I've never even been to therapy. And I'm not a child of divorce. My parents are still very much together and they very much want a grandchild to bear their name. In fact, there isn't a single divorce in my family (which isn't to say that there shouldn't have been). For better or worse, my only sister, both sets of grandparents, both sets of great-grandparents—

everybody got married and stayed that way. If that makes it sound like a predicament I suppose that's because I've often viewed it as such. A friend of mine, forty-four and single, says that getting married is like "breaking into prison to serve a life sentence." As pessimistic as that may sound, it betrays a sunny assumption: that they'll beat the roulette-level odds of actually staying together.

No, it doesn't take a cynic to be down on traditional matrimony these days. We all know the odds—roughly 50 percent of all American marriages will end in divorce and it's pretty much been that way since the second wave of feminism started leveling the sexual playing field in the 1970s. Of the 50 percent who stay together, you have to figure that at least some of them *should* get divorced, which effectively tips the scales in favor of marriage being an empirically bad idea. This isn't my opinion, it's math.

And yet while marriage rates have been dropping for the past forty years, and we're marrying later and later in life, the vast majority of Americans will choose to tie the knot by the time they're thirty-five. That's not a new trend at all: Marriage has been around for about four thousand years and it's always been very popular (if more volatile) among the young. What is a *relatively* new trend, however, is that almost all of these brides and grooms will marry for one reason, and one reason only:

True love.

We should indeed look back with pride at how far we've come as a culture since the days when marriage was a largely loveless, coercive institution, rooted in social, economic, and political practicality—and wifely subordination. But here we are at the dawn of a new millennium, enlightened, evolved, and yet the men look more like women, nobody has any pubic hair, and everybody's texting someone else as soon as you get up to go to the bathroom. It's like we're living in an Age of Ish—wireless, metro, and wishy-washy. We make soft plans to meet at ten-ish; sex columnist Dan Savage says the ideal modern marriage is "monogamish"; and that open-ended suffix has even become a word in itself.

"Are you a vegetarian?"

"Ish."

"Do you have a boyfriend?"

"Meh."

It's dizzying. We're connected 24/7 but eternally noncommittal, ever present and therefore never present, spending real time following fake friends whom we never, ever speak to and who wouldn't come to our funerals if they lived next to the cemetery. Meanwhile, we speak in euphemisms ("benefits"), emote with emoticons (*blush*), and we insist on making "'til death" decisions based on something as oxymoronic as *true love*.

What's the matter with us?

We all know the words to the songs: Love is *blind,* we *fall* in it—*madly*—*head over heels*. It's *bewitching*. A *battlefield*. An *infatuation*. It *stinks*. Cupid is *stupid,* we go *crazy* under his *spell,* getting *swept off our feet*—*weak in the knees*—going *gaga* like a baby. So what keeps us sitting on a bar stool with eternal optimism and wearing hookup underwear on blind dates? If we can't even walk and talk straight during the courtship phase, then how are we supposed to bring out the best in each other over a lifetime? How are we supposed to deal with meddling in-laws, underachieving toddlers, and months—maybe even years—without making out?

The most important question of all, then: How can we make sure our love is actually true *before* saying "I do"?

Some questions you can figure out for yourself. For others, you turn to those who know better. The people to whom I turned for answers knew best—they lived through it—and they shared their stories bravely and generously. I found my sources everywhere. Wherever I went there was always someone—or someone who knew someone—who was willing to be interviewed.

They're not "experts" or "gurus" or exhibitionist types looking to expand their following on Twitter. There was no glory to be gained, no revenge to be had, no money to be made. This is heart-to-heart, peer-to-peer sharing. The key to their candor: no real names (and all identifying details have been changed).

Most of them had never before spoken about their breakups in such gory detail and they found the process cathartic. One woman, from Wisconsin, described it as "the last dance with those demons." Others shut down and refused to revisit certain aspects of their past—and themselves. Some interviews were twenty minutes, some lasted more than eight hours, a few carried over for days. Five of these people are old friends of mine; two of them became friends; one woman I slept with (before the interview).

The material is divided into three sections—what I now consider to be the golden triangle of relationship advice: *Accelerating the Inevitable, Discussing the Dirty,* and *Engaging the Elephants.* While there's no panacea when it comes to matters of the heart, if you can apply these practices of self-actualization, sexual exploration, and verbal communication, respectively, there's a good chance you'll stay together. Or break up. Sometimes, I've learned, getting to "no" can be just as rewarding as getting to "yes."

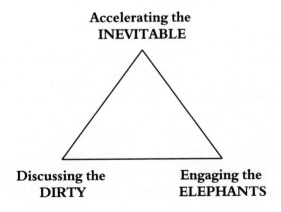

**Accelerating the
INEVITABLE**

**Discussing the
DIRTY**

**Engaging the
ELEPHANTS**

This book's title, *You Can Be Right (or You Can be Married),* comes from an early interview with a thirty-six-year-old woman who heard it, appropriately, from her stepmother. At first she thought it was "ludicrous," but the longer she was married, the more "right-on" she found it. To me, the saying has always meant that it's dangerous to prioritize the good of the individual over the good of the couple. Needing to be right requires proving the other person wrong, and that type of competitive "told ya so" thinking can be extremely divisive and demoralizing to a union.

It's getting late here on Cape Cod. I go upstairs to check on my grandma. She sleeps with a night-light next to her bed. I used to think it was because she was afraid of the dark—afraid of the spirits. But that isn't it at all; it's the opposite.

The better to see them with.

She's lying on her side of the bed with her mouth open and her eyes closed. I wait for her chest to move, proof that she's alive, and then head downstairs to the living room. I'm snooping again. On a shelf, I find a curious green book from 1927 called *About Ourselves: Psychology for Normal People* by H. A. Overstreet. In a chapter called "Halting the Expedition," he says that it's essential in a marriage to "face each other as equals, each cognizant of the necessity and dignity of the other's contribution." He explains how "the 'oneself' becomes 'ourselves,' and the 'I' becomes 'we two.'"

I like that: *we two.* It seems like a much more breathable existence than what God said in Genesis—that man should "cleave unto his wife and they shall become one flesh." But the real revelation comes on page forty-seven, where, pressed between two pages, I discover an actual, dried four-leaf clover (chances of mutation: roughly 1 in 10,000). According to Irish legend, the finder shall be showered with good fortune, each leaf representing, in order: faith, hope, love, and luck. I take it as an omen, then, that this particular clover is marking a poem written by Overstreet's friend who had apparently grown tired of the popular romantic authors of the day. Titled "Lines on Reading D. H. Lawrence, Sherwood Anderson, et al.," his plea (or protest) goes like this:

I

Friends, what's the matter with me?

II

I've been married eighteen years
And still love my wife.
I wonder what is the matter with me!

III

Judging from these books I'm told to read,
I ought to be tired of my wife;
But I'm not!
I ought to fall in love with another woman,
With other women,
With lots of other women;
But I don't!
Say, what's the matter with me?

The next morning I ask my grandma if it was she who marked the poem with the clover. She says she can't remember, but I like to believe it was. Or maybe it was my grandpa.

Incidentally, Sherwood Anderson, who published the novel *Many Marriages* in 1923, was married four times. And D. H. Lawrence, considered by many to be a pornographer at the time of his death, had a torrid affair with his professor's wife, with whom he eventually eloped. She was six years his senior, already a mother of three—and a translator of fairy tales!

Say, what's the matter with them?

That's what I've been trying to figure out. It's a mission that has raised a steady stream of concern from my family and friends. They regularly check in to inquire:

"Are you sure you really want to know all this stuff?"

"Why are you still single?"

"Don't you think writing a divorce book is gonna make you jaded?"

I don't think so. No, this really isn't a divorce book at all. What rises above the adultery and the acrimony is something much closer to courage. Sometimes it's the courage to stay and work things out; sometimes it's the courage to walk away. If I've learned one thing from this journey, it's that our capacity for debauchery and duplicity is matched only by our ability to forgive such transgressions and to find that pinprick of light in the dark. For better or worse, we're a nation of hopeful romantics.

This, then—paradoxically, perhaps—is a book about love.

ACCELERATING THE INEVITABLE

I want you to stop being subhuman and become "yourself."
"Yourself," I say. Not the newspaper you read,
not your vicious neighbor's opinion, but "yourself."
—WILHELM REICH

One should judge a man mainly from his depravities.
Virtues can be faked. Depravities are real.
—KLAUS KINSKI

He's not gonna change. He'll always be *him*.
—A middle-aged woman overheard
on her cell phone in Venice, California

As a teenager, before the Internet, I used to rummage through old notebooks when I couldn't sleep. Now I just Google stuff. Lately, I've been Googling what other people Google. I type in unfinished phrases just to see what comes up. For example, type "Will I ever" into the search bar, and according to Google's proprietary algorithms, these are the top three questions that are keeping others up at night:

Will I ever find love?
Will I ever get married?
Will I ever be good enough?

Type "I want to get" and you get the following:

I want to get pregnant.
I want to get married.
I want to get high.

Whatever this metadata reveals about the current state of altruism aside, it's clear that most people (the Googling kind, anyway) are most worried about winding up alone. Not surprisingly, then, the no. 1 question beginning with the phrase "Why am I" is:

Why am I still single?

I've been wondering the same thing. And to be blunt, I think it's because we're a nation of liars. Not the nefarious kind; we don't lie through our teeth. Instead, we grin and bear it, concealing our "flaws" and our "kinks," our heads moving easily between the clouds and the sand. It's a vicious cycle. If we want so badly to be loved for who we really are, then why do we build walls that prevent that from happening? If we strive for transparency, how do we wind up invisible?

"If you're afraid of loneliness," said Chekhov, "do not marry." Indeed, feeling like a stranger next to your spouse (or your girlfriend of three years) is a bit like living in solitary confinement. There's an instinct to climb the walls and place blame: "They don't get me, they don't see me." But I've learned through these interviews—and through my own failed relationships—that it's almost always our own fault.

The problem, I think, is that we get so giddy at the prospect of having found "the one" that we airbrush ourselves—and our partners—into a corner. Desperate to connect, we unwittingly self-sabotage through brazen acts of self-promotion, and like most forms of advertising, the pitch distorts the truth. Better to just be honest; every lie requires a lifetime of maintenance. What *really* turns you on? What *really* freaks you out? If it makes you feel any better, I'm fairly certain that nobody has ever actually bonded over a common love of Sunday brunches, strolls in the park, or *Kind of Blue*. We're not that cool. We're deeper than that. And hooking up to *Kind of Blue* is kind of boring.

"In a marriage, there's no hiding your complexity from the other person or the other person hiding their complexity from you," says Ruby. "Eventually all your shit comes out and it comes out in full force, so you might as well stop pretending sooner rather than later."

Were you meant for each other? There's only one way to find out. If you really want to love and be loved, you need to accelerate the inevitable and *just admit your shit*. Because it's all going to come out anyway. I'm paraphrasing Polonius, who advised his son:

> This above all: to thine own self be true,
> And it must follow, as the night the day,
> Thou canst not then be false to any man.

On this matter, there is no quibbling with the Bard (or with Ruby). I do, however, have a bone to pick with the guy who told us not to sweat the small stuff. I'm sorry, but I think that's terrible advice—it perpetuates the charade. At some fundamental level, we are what annoys us, so if something's bugging you, say it. *Nicely.* A man from Philadelphia told me, "Admit, don't accuse." Because the devil really *is* in the details, and I've learned that all those little letdowns that seem insignificant at the time can eventually creep up and kill you. Death by a thousand paper cuts is just as bloody as being stabbed in the back, and far more common. It's best to love with abandon, sure, but we can't abandon ourselves in the process. As my friend Marni says, "Don't paint the red flags white."

"The very best you can hope for is that you've got somebody who's gonna respect you enough to go through the day-to-day bullshit and be honest with you," says Jim.

"I wanted to be his perfect person at my own expense," says Liz.

"The human mind is a nimble thing," says Paul, "and we can tell ourselves stories to make the problematic stuff go away."

Unfortunately, no matter how hard we try to sell these stories, they'll never ring true and they'll never end happily. With 20/20 hindsight, everyone I spoke to agreed: Candor is the highest compliment. Before you can be one half of a duo, you need to be explicitly and wholeheartedly yourself. You can't dodge your DNA and change who you are to please someone else and nobody can do that for you. There's no valor in putting on a brave face—it's a mask like any other. You want to be a badass? Have the balls to be vulnerable.

Clearly, I don't have such balls. My friend Sarah agrees. I asked her to read this chapter and she called me afterward and said, "Listen, I think you should at least acknowledge the irony that you're encouraging people to be vulnerable in relationships, but you yourself have a hard time being vulnerable. I mean, I've been out with you. I know it was just one date, but you ask *a lot* of questions and reveal very little about yourself."

She's right. Why do I do that? What's *my* shit to admit? And is it character shit or behavior shit? Hopefully, it's behavioral; then maybe I can change it. And if I can, then maybe I won't be up Googling unfinished phrases in the middle of the night.

In the meantime, if you find yourself staring at a screen at 3 A.M., resist the urge to cyber stalk your exes and instead look up "Galway Kinnell, *Book of Nightmares*." What I've been trying to say, Mr. Kinnell said better in just six words:

Let our scars fall in love.

"It's not a question of winning love from people. It's either there or it isn't—there's nothing you can do other than be yourself."

ALIAS: Liz

OCCUPATION: Mom

YEAR OF BIRTH: 1970

CURRENT MARRIAGE STATUS: Divorced

DO YOU HAVE ANY CHILDREN? One nine-year-old

WHERE YOU GREW UP: Wisconsin

WHERE YOU LIVE: Virginia

YEAR OF MARRIAGE: 2002

HOW LONG YOU DATED BEFORE YOU WERE MARRIED: Two years

YEAR OF DIVORCE: 2007

Whoever somebody shows themselves to be right at the beginning, that's who they are. Your very first impression, you're usually right. *Listen, listen, listen* to that.

I remember, right at the beginning of our relationship, we'd gone to Barcelona. It was this crazy weekend. I was in my bikini and we ended up having mad sex in the hotel pool. And he said to me, "Will you remember this when you hate me?" And I remember thinking, "I will *never*. How could I ever hate you?"

It comes back to me sometimes, that memory. Because I can't believe how I got to the point where I actually have hated him. And he predicted that right at the beginning.

It's not a question of winning love from people. It's either there or it isn't—there's nothing you can do other than be yourself. The problem is that you meet somebody and you start falling for them and you see the person they want you to be and there's this fantastic satisfaction in becoming that person. There's something very female about that, being able to metamorphosize yourself into an ideal that fulfills someone else's desire.

But it's all a game. Six months into the relationship you suddenly go, "Actually, you need to know that I can't cope with that" or "I need this" or "I'm not good at this." And they're just shocked because you haven't shown *any* of that. And that's when you realize that you haven't been truthful. And it's your responsibility entirely.

I've had this discussion with so many of my female friends: How the fuck do you remain truthful when you desire somebody that much? Or when you really want something to work? I did that with my husband to the nth—just ticked all the boxes. I wanted to be his perfect person at my own expense. So finally when I turned around and went, "I'm not happy," he said, "Excuse me, *what*? You're not happy? But you're my rock!"

The most interesting thing that came out of counseling was when the therapist said, "She's your rock, yes, but do you see how incredibly fragile she is?" At which point I immediately burst into tears. And he just looked staggered. He hadn't seen it because I hadn't shown it. Why? I think women are fundamentally afraid of being needy. Particularly strong, independent women. You fear that need is simply seen as weakness and that it'll be rejected.

I remember having this argument with a group of friends about how we're not used to integrating vulnerability into our relationships and about how we determine the difference between *want* and *need*. My closest female friend was there, and she's the strongest woman I've ever known, and she said, "I'm not ashamed to say that I need my husband. And I will call him and say, 'I need you now,' and I know he's gonna come. I know he's gonna sit there like a nodding dog and listen to me, and hold me, and he may not say a word, but I'll feel better." And all the men around the table went pale at the word "need." We said, "What's wrong with 'need'?" And they said, "We don't like the word 'need.' We like the word 'want.' *I want you—I want you now.* That's fantastic, that's sexy."

20

* * *

There was a piece in the *New York Times Magazine* called "The Happy Marriage Is the 'Me' Marriage" that I thought was really on the money. The "me" marriage is where you say, "This is me and these are my needs." You're both completely transparent about that and you come together in what you can do mutually. The idea is that if you allow each other to have lives outside of the relationship then you'll have everything to bring back *into* the relationship. It has to do with Venn diagrams. The Venn diagram that's interlinked at the core, that's good, that's sustainable. But the Venn diagram that overlaps entirely, one over the other, that's not sustainable—that's an eclipse. If the relationship becomes too codependent or too symbiotic, it implodes.

Now, my upbringing is to be the person that grounds somebody else. Because I'm calm and I'm rational and I analyze and I'm very good when people come to me in a crisis. I become the person that makes somebody else feel safe. And that happens quite quickly because I think I'm maternal. But what I forget— and what my partners forget—is that I can't endlessly be somebody's rock if there's no rock for me. It's that whole "radiate or drain" scenario. You suddenly get to a point in your life when you realize that unless you're being nurtured, you cannot nurture. You realize that your reserves aren't endless and that to lead a full life and be free and creative you have to be with someone who is as excited by you as you are by them. It's got to be a reciprocal process.

Unconditional love, you have that with your children. In my love for my daughter I have a freedom to be myself that I haven't had in any other relationship. We can be angry with each other, we can cry, we can tell each other we love each other every day. Nothing is cheesy, nothing gets old. It's all part of a mutual betterment that is a complete togetherness. But with adults in a relationship, it's not like that. That type of love isn't given; it's

21

earned. You can say "I love you" a hundred and ten times and it doesn't mean anything. It's in how you *are,* how you treat somebody, what you do for them. It's not what you say to them, it's not empty gestures. It's just somebody knowing that you genuinely have their back. That's love.

"You have to put everything on the table. If you don't, that's not fair to the other person because you have to at least give them the *chance* to love all those 'off' things about you."

ALIAS: Ann

OCCUPATION: Nonprofit

YEAR OF BIRTH: 1972

CURRENT MARRIAGE STATUS: Divorced

DO YOU HAVE ANY CHILDREN? Two boys, eight years old and five
    years old

WHERE YOU GREW UP: Georgia

WHERE YOU LIVE: New York

YEAR OF MARRIAGE: 2001

HOW LONG YOU DATED BEFORE YOU WERE MARRIED: Five years

YEAR OF DIVORCE: 2012

In high school, I liked my looks, but I didn't know that other people did. I was never the hot girl. I was told, "When you grow up, you'll be pretty." Boys liked me, but I thought it was because I was nicer than most girls. I don't know what was going on with me, but up until my marriage, I only liked the guys who weren't that into me. The good guys, I'd get bored so fast.

Chris and I met at a restaurant. He had just moved to New York, but he started working immediately as an actor. I'd been waiting tables for four and a half years so I was like, "Wow, he's on it!" I was surprised I started falling for him because he was so clean-cut and beautiful, and that was never attractive to me. But I could see that he was talented, and every time he came around, he was just so *nice*. And he didn't have that New York, actory, pessimistic sense of humor where everybody's too cool, just going *pfft, pfft*. He liked all these cheesy, romantic songs that to me were like *blech*. I couldn't believe I was going gaga over a guy who was playing "The Dance" by Garth Brooks on guitar in front of me. But he was doing it, singing, and I was like, "Aww! What a sweet soul!" He just seemed so wholesome, so pure.

God, I'll never be that dumb again.

At first I didn't know what the cracks were, or that they'd been there since before we got married. Any problem, I just automatically turned it on myself. I always thought there was something wrong with *me*—some insecurity—like, maybe if I did *this* better, everything would be okay. Because any time I tried to talk to him about something that was bothering me, he would do the whole: "What are you talking about? Are you nuts?" So I was like: "Okay, I must be bat-shit crazy." Then I'd be embarrassed because I looked insecure.

I sound so retarded—*so* retarded—but I found underwear that wasn't mine: twice. The first time, our housekeeper goes, "Uh, are these yours?" She knew damn well they weren't mine. And I was like, "Huh? Let me see them." But I just covered it up immediately: "Oh, those must be Tina's. She always has people over when we're out of town."

It happened again a few years later. We were living in an apartment and I found a pair of beautiful, black, lace, tiny underwear. And I was like, "Holy shit, how did these get in here? Oh, they must have gotten mixed up with somebody's laundry." That's what I thought: "It can't be Chris, he's made it so clear that he can't even *think* about another woman besides me." Looking back, I think I just didn't want to know the truth.

There were a few times throughout our marriage when I would come home and say, "Just be real with me. Be really *real* with me. What's going on? I can see that you're miserable and you don't want to be. Just tell me the truth and we'll see if we can fix it." But again, he would act like that was crazy of me.

Why? It's simple: If you're with a lying, cheating son of a bitch, they'll always try to flip it around because they don't want to get found out. So, ladies, if anybody's trying to make *you* feel crazy, they're probably fucking someone behind your back.

It was heartbreaking, the way I found out about everything. He was shooting a movie on location. It was a big, intense role. I was home with the kids. For the first part of the shoot, he kept in contact but I could see him turning into a weirdo, being really distant, thinking they're doing this heavy shit that's gonna blow some minds, y'know? Like, "Oh, you wouldn't understand." Like they're making *Apocalypse Now*. It was creeping me out. I just wanted to go, "Dude, it's a fucking movie. It's a bunch of hot people in makeup. *Relax*."

Our video chats got to the point where he was just, "Uh-huh. Uh-huh." As if he didn't want to be there. So I thought, "Okay, I'll just leave him alone until he gets done with this character." But when he came home, something felt wrong. They had to dye his hair for the movie and the first thing he wanted to do was dye his hair again. He was like, "It's just fucking gray, I'm looking old." And I was like, "It looks *good*. It's gonna look weird to dye it."

All of a sudden, he was really concerned with wearing "cool" clothes. He kept calling it *Williamsburg*. He wanted to dress *Williamsburg*y. And he went shopping the next day and got skinny jeans. Like, now he's Mr. Grit, y'know? And he started listening to "cool" music, too, and that was pissing me off because that's the kind of music *I* like, and he always used to say, "That has no melody." Then he's saying, "Hey, check this out, have you ever heard of Animal Collective?" And I was like, "Yeah, I know, I played it for you a year ago!"

He was just acting like an asshole. Nothing felt true. And then I started getting that bad feeling. It was *burning*. One night we were in the kitchen and I just went, "Oh, my God, Chris, are you having an affair?"

He slumped into the kitchen counter and said, "Really? You think after all this time being married we're not going to have feelings for someone else?"

I was pretty sure who it was, they'd worked together on the movie. So I asked him: "Was it . . . ?"

"Well . . ."

"Did you kiss her?"

"No, it was just this emotional connection . . ."

I started crying. "I'm so sorry you had to go to her to get your emotional needs met. I always told you that you could talk to me about anything." He was clearly annoyed that we were even having this conversation. But I said, "I think we need to call a therapist."

He went, "I think you're going a little overboard with this."

And I was like, "I don't care. Even if it *is* nothing, we need to start dealing with *us* because something isn't right. Something hasn't been right for a really long time."

At this point I didn't even think he'd fucked her—or anybody else. I didn't even think he'd *kissed* her. I was so insecure, I started thinking that, somehow, this was all my fault. I must have done something to make him so unhappy. I thought maybe I was hideous-looking. Or that maybe I was walking around with a faulty vagina. So I went to my gynecologist and I said, "Look at it. Test it out. Is it in working order?" I thought maybe I needed to get one of those surgeries down there [laughs]. But he said it was fine. And then I went to my girlfriend, who is bisexual, and I was like, "Look at it." And she was like, "You're fine!" And then she dropped her pants and said, "Look, they're all different." And hers did a weird thing, but it was fine, too [laughs].

So Chris and I went to the therapist. And the whole time he was acting like, "This is ridiculous." We went back home and he had to leave the next day for a photo shoot in LA. And that's when I started thinking, "I'm gonna do something so crazy when he's gone."

* * *

I was getting ready to snoop but I wasn't sure how to do it. I never knew his password; I wouldn't even think to ask. So after he left for the shoot, I called him, all frantic, like, "Oh, shit! School just called and I need to print out some pictures for something. Can I have your password?"

And he was like, "Uh, but . . ."

"Just give it real quick."

"Well, you could use . . ."

"No, no—this is faster."

I did a good job. Real savvy. And that's how I saw all the e-mails between him and her. I just typed in the first letter of her name and there they were. He was telling her about how he'd been feeling *dead* and *lifeless* the last decade, and how now, *finally,* he knows what *true passion* is. He said he felt like he'd been *strapped onto a rocket and launched into space.* Oh, and get this, one of the notes said, *I actually went to therapy with Ann today. I think she's onto something. I'm not sure. I can't believe I'm spending five hundred dollars an hour to talk to someone when you at twenty-seven years old have more wisdom than anybody I have ever met.*

More wisdom? *What?* It was awful. My legs didn't work. I couldn't hear. My hands closed up, and my feet. I couldn't open them. It was like I'd just watched someone get killed right in front of me. I was just going, "No, no, no," staring at the words on the screen.

I called his best friend and asked him if he would come over. I said, "Matt, I found e-mails and I'm so scared. What does this mean? Is he in love with her?"

He said, "I can't talk to you about this. You're going to have to talk to your girlfriends."

And I was like, "What the fuck? You knew?!"

He knew.

My body went into shock. I couldn't eat. I couldn't drink. It hurt so bad. I called my friend Lynne and said, "Buy a pack of cigarettes." I had quit smoking two years before. So she came over, I got on to Chris's other computer, his laptop, and that's where I found all these photos of them in bed together, all cozy and kissing. What I just hated—and what stuck with me for so long— were the pictures he took of her looking like a tortured, beautiful soul. That whole bit, like, *Oh, don't look at me.* There was one of her sitting outside the hotel room with their dirty sheets in a ball, like, *oopsy daisy*! But it was no accident at all; they knew exactly what they were doing. It felt like they were laughing at me.

So I called him. He was in LA at the shoot. I told him, "I found the e-mails and I saw the pictures."

He said, "Ann, stop reading them."

I said, "Okay. I'm sorry."

But I didn't stop reading them. I forwarded them to myself and to my friend. Because I knew he'd erase them and I didn't want to be able to talk myself out of what I'd seen. I was like, "Keep seeing this. You need to keep seeing this."

Everything fully came out around New Year's, on the way to our second therapy session. We were driving and I said, "Have you ever been with anyone before this? Or is this the only time?"

He said, "Four or five others."

I couldn't even react anymore. I said, "There's got to be more. How can I try to fix something if I don't know the whole truth? Give me the whole truth so I can know if I can deal with it. Plus, when we go to these stupid shindigs, if one of these chicks sits in my lap and starts falling all over me, I need to know if she's fucked you or not."

So on New Year's Day he gave me the list—about forty names. One girl got pregnant; he had to pay for an abortion. Another one was one of my best friends. I was her maid of honor. She was at our wedding. I remember them singing "You're the One That I Want" together, and I was just thinking, "Oh, there's crazy Lexi humping my husband! What a funny gal!"

Yeah, I was scared. I mean, how could he keep all those secrets? I couldn't even *count* them. And he was doing it even before we got married, when we were living together, and that made me doubly mad, like, You didn't *have* to marry me. And then when we got married, he didn't stop. He kept going. I guess you kind of have to admire it in a way. Like wow, he really is good at something. He has a true gift—for lying.

At that point nothing would have shocked me, so I had to ask him, for real: "Have you ever killed anybody? Accidentally or anything? Have you ever raped anyone? Have you fucked a man? Are you a pedophile? Did you ever sleep with my sister or my cousin? Just tell me the truth."

I was destroyed, and I was mad, but then I started thinking, "You know what? This must be hard for him, too. He's got to have so much guilt. Let him process it, give him a chance to do the work he needs to do. Maybe this is a chance for us." I told him, "If you come clean about everything, we can deal with it. But you have to help me. If you can walk me through this, we'll just keep on walking, together."

I was so willing. But he couldn't do it. And I got tired. I made plans to go to Palm Springs. Before I left, I said, "I'm afraid I'm going to have to let you go. I don't want to let you go, but I will if I have to."

He said, "Do whatever you have to do to be happy."

And that's what it took. I went to Palm Springs, did a ceremony for myself, let him go, came back, and said, "I want a divorce." And it felt so good. I agonized over that for the longest time. But then I really came alive.

You know when you're a kid, like eight years old, and nothing's gone wrong yet, everything's pure, and you feel like, "Oh, God, I can do anything"? That's how I feel again. I just feel right— more like myself now than ever—and I don't want to make the same mistakes ever again: being scared to see the whole picture.

From now on, I'm only gonna love full-on, huge, and no games. I want to be completely transparent, through and through. It's like I have truth Tourette's. Even when I think, "Oh, no, this is not a good side of me, this is an embarrassing side, this could be icky"—I'm not going to act like it's not there. I always fought being jealous. Now, when I feel jealous, I just say it right away. I don't even know what it is, necessarily, but I'll just announce it to the person I'm with, and then I backtrack, trying to figure out why.

I'm through being a "cool" girl. I'm going to show it all, and I want someone who's going to be that real with me. I know now that you have to put everything on the table. If you don't, that's not fair to the other person because you have to at least give them the *chance* to love all those "off" things about you. And if you can fall in love being completely who you are, that sounds like the best thing ever. I've never had that, but I know that's what I want. If I end up being alone, so be it. But I don't want to fake anything ever, ever, ever again.

"You have to find somebody who is willing to accept you for who you are and then tell you that that's not good enough. And with their help, you figure out how to be better. And you need to do the same thing for them."

ALIAS: Jim

OCCUPATION: Editor

YEAR OF BIRTH: 1960

CURRENT MARRIAGE STATUS: Married to my third and current wife
since 1998

DO YOU HAVE ANY CHILDREN? A nineteen-year-old and a sixteen-year-
old from my second marriage, a seven-year-old and a three-year-old from
my third

WHERE YOU GREW UP: Pennsylvania

WHERE YOU LIVE: New Jersey

YEAR OF MARRIAGE: 1983, 1994, 1998

HOW LONG YOU DATED BEFORE YOU WERE MARRIED: Seven years,
two years, one and a half years

YEAR OF DIVORCE: 1990, 1997

There's no such thing as a Noël Coward divorce. You know, that sort of amicable, happy-go-lucky divorce where everybody's interested in pursuing their own interests and whatever maliciousness there is is sort of cleverly and beautifully executed. It's not like that at all. I don't care how much you might have loved the person, halfway through any divorce the only thing you can think of is, *I hate this person and I want this person to bleed.* You become *obsessed*. It becomes a matter of absolute survival. Once it's over, the question is not whether you can recover from the love, or from the *loss* of love. It's whether or not you can get over your own hatred. And I've been divorced twice, okay?

The first time it was a very casual marriage. We met in college in 1977. We really had very little in common but we enjoyed each other's company. We were both quasi-romantic young actors. Well, I was an actor, she was a writer, and we had adopted this whole self-consciously bohemian lifestyle. We kind of drifted *together*. A series of one-night stands kept getting closer and closer and the next thing we knew one of us didn't go home anymore.

This went on for a while until all of a sudden we had no money and the coffeemaker broke. And we figured, what the fuck, why not get married? Somebody will give us a coffeemaker. And they did. They gave us a coffeemaker and they gave us a popcorn maker. And we fought like cats and dogs over that fuckin' coffeemaker and that fuckin' popcorn maker. And you know what? I don't eat popcorn and she didn't drink coffee [laughs]!

Look, I'll be perfectly honest with you—I was flat-out the world's worst husband. I was inconsiderate, I was selfish, I was utterly self-absorbed. On the rare occasions that we did have any money, if I wanted to spend some, I would. Now, at this period in time, I was also a drunk. And on November 19, 1983, I went on an absolutely horrific bender. And in the course of that bender, I slapped her.

Understand, not a month before that, I had been arrested for drunk driving. I had been thrown in the worst hole that Luzerne County, Pennsylvania, had to offer. It was this nineteenth-century prison where I was left with a fellow inmate who would've cut off my finger to get my ring, okay? *That* didn't sober me up. But when I understood that I had slapped my wife, that did. And that was enough to make me stop drinking.

But you know what my stopping drinking did? It destroyed my marriage. Because we no longer had anything in common. Actually, I have to credit her with my becoming a writer because in an effort to hold the marriage together I pretty much gave up the whole actor-playwright thing. We moved down to the Jersey Shore and I started working at a small weekly newspaper. This was 1985, I was twenty-seven old. I would go in at nine-thirty on Monday morning, and no bullshit, I'd work straight through until about 2 A.M. Wednesday morning. The upshot of all this was that my wife and I now no longer even had contact. We hardly ever saw each other.

To be perfectly honest, I think the reason I was doing it was because there really wasn't anything to come home to. This went on for about a year and a half. It was around this time that a really young reporter who came from a really troubled background started hitting on me. And I responded. It never got to the point of sex because frankly I was too conflicted to have it. But it came very, very close, and the sexual tension was utterly addictive, particularly for a recovering alcoholic. I became addicted to the guilt, the shame, the anger. . . . Meanwhile, I made very little effort to hide any of this from my wife. And at that point, she entered into a similar relationship with a guy.

Now, it was interesting because I couldn't be as magnanimous and open-minded as she had been, and this led to her saying she wanted out of the marriage. So now, all of a sudden, all of this ambivalence we had had for all these years suddenly ossified and became a molten core of rage. When you look at the papers filed in this no-fault divorce in the state of New Jersey, it is a collection of every misstep, every error, every horrible thing that either of us did in the then twelve years we had known each other. I would put something in and she would respond with something. Then I would get so outraged that I would respond with something else. It was *vicious*. It really was a blood sport.

Understand, nothing that I ever did during the course of our entire marriage involved me thinking about her as a first thought. And yet now, as we were going through the divorce, she was all I could think about. We were separated, but I knew where her boyfriend lived, and I would find myself making a point of going out of my way to drive past his apartment so I could see whether or not her car was there. It was all-consuming. If there had been one-tenth—one-*hundredth*—as much passion in our marriage as there was in our divorce, we would have just celebrated our twenty-fifth wedding anniversary.

My second marriage failed in spite of—but I think in part *because*—I tried to not make the same mistakes I made in my first marriage. But what I did was, except for the alcohol, I married the me of 1977. Irresponsible, self-centered, obsessive, destructive. She was artistic, she was a musician and a writer. She was sexually aggressive. *Phenomenally* aggressive. And sure enough, everything that I did to my first wife, she did to me.

Yes, I did feel that there was a certain karmic retribution in all of this. But here's the thing, and it took me three times to figure this out. You have to find somebody who is willing to accept you for who you are and then tell you that that's not good enough. And with their help, you figure out how to be better. And you need to do the same thing for them. But if you're not willing to turn around and say, "I accept, I demand, and I work," then you're not willing to be married.

What's present in my marriage now that wasn't present in the other two is respect. I pitied one and I had an accommodation with the other. But I didn't respect either of them and they didn't respect me. And that's the most important thing. The very best you can hope for is that you've got somebody who's gonna respect you enough to go through the day-to-day bullshit and be honest with you. That's the most romantic thing in the world.

There is something absolutely *divine*—I mean, literally, the breath of God—in the ability to put someone else in your heart, to think of them first. But from the time of the greatest pornographer who ever lived, Shakespeare, we've demanded that love be something more. No, fuck Shakespeare—since the *Song of Songs*! And what happens is, the utter grandeur and magnificence of what love actually *is* gets overshadowed by this disappointment that it's not the way we fantasized it *should* be.

Now, that's not a new phenomon. The *new* phenomenon is

the ability to divorce *easily*. You asked me before how you know when it's over. That question is almost irrelevant now because most of us never get that far to find out. Half of us are out the door as soon as it starts to fall apart. And we go to marriage counselors, whose job it is to make the decision for us and then make us think we made it ourselves. So we never really get to the point, as a culture, where we have to ask that question: Should this marriage be saved or should it be discarded? Because our predilection is just to discard it.

It's not a moral thing. It's not a character thing. Whenever you give people an opportunity not to be in pain, they're gonna take it. And the lower you set the threshold, the earlier they're gonna take it. I wonder, then, whether we might not have made divorce a little *too* easy.

And here's the point—it's *crucial* in all this. It's goddamn easy to file for divorce, okay? It's goddamn easy to be *declared* divorced. But those eighteen months between those two actions—man, those are the hardest eighteen months of your fucking life.

"You need to reserve the right to get angry. Holding it in only wreaks havoc on your body."

ALIAS: Debbie

OCCUPATION: Social worker

YEAR OF BIRTH: 1970

CURRENT MARRIAGE STATUS: Divorced

DO YOU HAVE ANY CHILDREN? No

WHERE YOU GREW UP: Maryland

WHERE YOU LIVE: Maryland

YEAR OF MARRIAGE: 2003

HOW LONG YOU DATED BEFORE YOU WERE MARRIED: Four
   years

YEAR OF DIVORCE: 2008

Is it hard for you to talk about this?

It's not something I talk about often but clearly a lot of people know. I have very close friends and a close family. But it's really based on trust and the knowledge that they're not going to judge me. This is a part of my life, it's a part of who I am, but by no means does it define me.

How did you lose your license as a clinical social worker?

The main rule of thumb is "do no harm." And I did harm because I abused my power. There are certain ethics and laws that we have to abide by and one of them is not to have any kind of sexual relationship with a client. So I not only did harm to this man and to my husband and to our friends and families, but to all the people I worked with who trusted me. My supervisor, I haven't spoken to her since. She's still my role model and I'm still learning from her, and it's very, very sad that I'll never have a relationship with her again.

Was it an elaborate affair?
Oh, yeah. Two cell phones. My parents, to this day, they look back on it and say, "How did you live with yourself when you went home after being with this man? How did you have such a dangerous affair?"

Why was it so dangerous?
One, because I knew he was a felon. He'd been to jail several times for assault and battery and for dealing drugs—crack cocaine. And it was dangerous because he was a sociopath, so what would stop him from killing me? Literally. What would stop him from hurting my family?

Let's back up a bit so we can understand what was going on in your marriage at the time. Tell me about your ex-husband. How did you two meet?
I was twenty-seven. I'm going to refer to him as Voldemort, okay? So Voldemort was working at a summer camp in South Carolina and my friend was the director of the camp. They'd gone to graduate school together and she said, "You have to meet him." We were both planning trips to the Middle East and I was a little nervous to be going on my own so we met and we made a plan to meet in Cairo.

Would you describe yourself as a strong, independent person?
It's funny, people just assumed, "Wow, you have all this courage, you're strapping on this backpack and going—you strong woman, you." But really, no. I thought I was supposed to do it because other people I knew had done it. The truth is, I wasn't very self-assured at all.

So the second time you ever saw Voldemort was in Cairo?
Yeah. We traveled around for the next seven months. But I

remember arguing with him even then. People look back on a marriage and say, "Oh, there was that time when things were just so easy." It was *never* easy.

Did you ever feel like it was fate or destiny that brought you together?
There was definitely that mentality of: Maybe this was meant to be. It's kind of cliché, but on paper, we were the perfect couple. Two Jews meet in Cairo. My parents are from DC; his parents are from DC. He loves the outdoors and I love the outdoors. Perfect! We just thought, "If it works on paper, it should work in real life."

Was there a strong physical attraction?
Yeah, initially. He's smart, good-looking, and he has a beautiful smile. In most of my previous relationships, I felt that I was put on a bit of a pedestal. But not with him, and for some reason that was attractive. I can't say that it was great sex, though. It was never an "I can't keep my hands off you" kind of relationship.

Did you click intellectually? Was it ever an "I can't stop talking to you" kind of a relationship?
From very early on we were fighting. It's interesting that my mind goes right to the fighting. And there's definitely blame to be had on both sides. But I think I always had the mind-set that he may change and he may learn how to express his opinions so we're able to have a conversation and I don't feel shut out of the dialogue. It was always with that hope: *It'll get better.* And maybe there was also a desperation on my part. A fear of being alone. I was twenty-seven, I wanted to be in a relationship.

Was there a lot of excitement in that getting-to-know-you phase? Were you genuinely interested in learning from—and about—each other?

I liked learning from him but I don't think he was so curious to learn from me. And he didn't really respect what I did for a living. "Social workers, psychologists—they're all crazy," he'd say. And it's like, "Um, I'm a fucking social worker!"

Who said "I love you" first?
I did. We were in Yosemite, camping. And he said, "Thank you." I thought, "Okay, he's not ready to tell me he loves me." Or maybe he *didn't* love me yet. I remember saying it at different times in our relationship and then asking, "Why don't you ever say it back?" Or, "You don't often tell me you love me. Why?" His response would be, "I don't feel like I need to say it often" or some cliché about actions speaking louder than words. But a girl needs to know.

Did he ever tell you what he loved about you?
I really didn't know what he loved about me. Sometimes he would say, "I don't get it, I introduce you to my friends and they're like, *Oh, she's great, she's great.* But I feel like I don't get the great you." And I think he was right. Because we didn't bring out the best in each other. Even at our actual wedding. The night before I kind of joked with him: "You wrote your vows, right?" The next day we're under the huppah and I read mine to him. Then, in this way that he thought was cute and playful, he took my vows and read them back to me. I was really disappointed. I remember someone coming up to me after and asking, "Did you know he was going to do that?"

Were you having second thoughts on your wedding day?
I can picture us dancing around and celebrating and having fun but it wasn't like we were celebrating *together.* I remember thinking, "Something is not quite right."

Looking back now, do you have any idea what that "something" was?

I think he had very specific things that he was looking for in a wife. The person had to enjoy being in nature. They had to be Jewish. Not materialistic. So I had to fit into a certain slot. I had to mold myself. So how do you show who you really are if you feel like you always have to be a certain way? For example, if I felt anxious or depressed, he'd just be like, "Snap out of it!" Or, "Go out and be in nature and then you'll feel better." But I had a much more serious problem than that. Clinical depression isn't something you can just snap yourself out of. So at some point I didn't feel safe being myself. And he didn't like the anxious me, so that became very difficult.

He didn't believe in depression?
I don't think so. And I don't fault him for not understanding it. But to not want to learn about it because it was going to make his wife happier? I would ask him to read *one chapter* in a book that I had but he never even picked it up.

You were living in hope? Thinking, *It'll get better?*
Yeah, or delusion—thinking that things weren't as bad as they were. I think one of the things that happens when you're in an unhappy marriage is that you just accept it. *We're settled; this is as good as it gets.* Divorce never crossed my mind. I didn't let it.

Did the sex get better as you were together?
No, it was better in the beginning. It was more frequent. I didn't have to concentrate to have an orgasm. But then it became . . . maybe it was a loss of my libido. I didn't *desire* him. It was mechanical. It wasn't experimental or interesting. And I didn't feel like when we weren't in bed that we were having a warm, loving relationship. Laying around together. The things that make sex better is all that time during the day, all the little affection, just being touched by somebody. There's nothing quite as good as sitting on the couch and someone wants you to hold them.

Did you feel needed?
I remember standing in our apartment and having an argument and I told him I wanted him to need me. And his response was one of self-reliance: "I don't need anybody." To my core, I need to be needed. That's one of the reasons why I became a social worker. And I'm not ashamed of the need to be needed.

Did he associate need with neediness? With weakness?
He never said that, but yes. And depression is weakness. And relying on things that aren't organic. Like shopping or getting your hair colored or getting your nails done.

Were you able to fight fairly and productively, where both people felt heard? Or was it more about being right or winning?
I think he looked at a world that was much more black and white. There was a right way and a wrong way. So when he expressed his opinion, it was the *right* way.

Did you have big fights? Yelling and screaming?
Yeah, we had big fights. I would yell. I didn't know how to express myself in a way that would make him listen, so I got angry. I would lose my temper and that was an ugly me. I remember once he looked in my closet and made some typical remark about my values, being materialistic or whatever. I said, "Fuck you." I remember trembling when the words came out. Not because I never say "fuck," I rather like the word. But I think the trembling comes from an inability to express anger. It's a complicated emotion. But you need to reserve the right to get angry. Holding it in only wreaks havoc on your body.

Were you trying to hurt or humiliate each other?
No. I think we were both deeply frustrated. I don't think either of us had the courage or the guts to say, "This is done, this is wrong." Maybe because we were both always thinking about the

relationship on paper. But we just weren't in love anymore. I don't know when that happened. I cared about him, I worried about him, I wanted him to be happy, healthy. But all of those things don't mean you're in love.

Why did you stay for as long as you did?
Same reason many people do. To avoid being alone. Although I *was* alone.

How long into the marriage did you start having the affair?
About four years.

How did it happen?
I was working for a program where we had a drop-in shelter for homeless people, drug addicts. We'd roll out beds every night. I built relationships with these men and women that I never thought possible. And my supervisor, she thought I was great. And I remember thinking, "Wow, I wish Voldemort could see me at my best."

So as things were deteriorating at home you were getting acknowledgment and validation at work?
Yes. I would walk into this center and I was given the time of day. And I think this man saw that. *Everybody loves her.* He was one of the first clients that I interviewed there, and I was, like, "Wow, he wants therapy?"

He was homeless?
Yes.

And a drug addict?
He was a drinker. He was allowed to drink and do drugs and continue to sleep at the shelter. Everybody who came there was. So I met him and he was absolutely everything that I would

never . . . like, I had no fantasy about being with a black man. It was just . . . the *attention*. The way he looked at me. He was charming. And I think I was really lifted up by how well I was doing in my job.

What did he look like?
Attractive, in some ways. In some ways, no. Shaved head. No piercings, no tattoos. Average. He had a belly because he was an alcoholic.

How old?
Fifty-one.

Smart?
Not smart. Clever. Streetwise. Charismatic. Manipulative. Manipulative more than smart or clever. There was a reason why he was still alive.

When did the boundaries begin to blur?
Pretty early on he was like, "Let's go have coffee." And I was like, "No, this is a therapeutic relationship. We don't go have coffee. I'm not your friend, I'm your therapist." And I would try to set the boundaries. But then maybe we would meet for more than one hour. Or I remember the first time he said he had a restless night. He said he was thinking about me.

Were you flattered?
Yeah. I mean, it's a visceral feeling. I didn't feel that way around Voldemort. He didn't make me *hot*.

What kind of stories was he telling you in those early therapy sessions?
Oh, the stories I'm thinking of were just really nasty. He would tell me when he was with other women. But it was almost in

a violent way. Like, he would give me details about how he would be giving a woman oral sex, and let's say she would have an orgasm, he would demand that she come twice. And if she didn't, he'd get angry. So that is disgusting, of course. But when you're sitting in a small room with this person and you have no excitement in your own sex life, that anger and passion, it all feels like the same thing.

It was a turn-on?
Yes, it kind of was. You feel it.

When did it turn sexual between you two?
After a lot of pushing, I agreed to meet him in the morning by the park. And then that became more frequent. And then finally he was like, "Let's go to a motel." And I was like, "I'll think about it." And then I remember, I said, "Yes." And then I quickly was like, "I change my mind." But there was no changing my mind. I'd signed up. So we got a motel room. It was probably ten o'clock in the morning. No talking, just sex. And at that moment I had never felt so good in my life.

What made it feel so good?
It was partly just the physical climax. I went back there the next morning. I couldn't say no to him.

What kinds of sexual things did you do together?
Well, I knew that he wasn't able to get a full erection so we never had sexual intercourse. It was pretty much about him pleasing me. But the only way he would be pleased is if I was pleased over and over again. I felt like I had to climax or I would get hurt. There was that feeling when I was with him that I *had* to. I was being *forced* to. I mean, it wasn't rape because I said *okay* but there was still that sense of *I have to do this*.

44

Did that add to it?
Sometimes, yeah. And we would have sex in all sorts of places. In stairwells. In motel rooms. In my car—*during the day*.

Always just oral?
Yes, correct. And even though he couldn't get a full erection, he could still come. No chance of me getting pregnant because he couldn't come inside me.

He could come from masturbating?
Or in my mouth. And I would have to do it, to completion, even if it took a really long fucking time.

Was that a turn-on as well?
No. That was survival.

So what kept you coming back for more?
It was like crack cocaine. You know it's bad for you but you keep going back and doing it. Because I wasn't getting that excitement anywhere else. So maybe I wasn't "doing drugs" but I *was* doing drugs because it controlled me.

Did the affair seep into your real life?
Yes. He would call me incessantly on my cell phone and leave messages that were really graphic. Like, "You're probably sucking your husband's dick," and "You're a kike" or "You're a Jewish cunt"—that was a big one for him.

Why did you put up with that?
What I put up with, none of it made any sense. But I think it really spoke to how unhappy I was during that period.

Did you ask if he had any STDs?
I don't think I asked him.

Really?

I really don't know. It's like telling war stories. I mean, how *did* I do those things? It's just unimaginable. I had a major fucking meltdown. I was, in psychological terms, totally dissociated. I went against every moral code that I believe in. I can remember looking in the mirror and not identifying with what I saw. I just completely became all these different people. My wife self. My whore self. My friend self. And I was also my work self.

What was your "wife self" doing back at home during all this?

The only way for me to relax was to drink beer and cook dinner. I don't remember sitting down. I'd cook and I'd clean and I'd fuss around with whatever and never really stop. I just remember moving. And when I would go to bed, I'd just fall right to sleep. It didn't keep me up at night.

Did this man think that you were going to leave your husband for him?

No, but he was afraid that I was going to get pregnant [by my husband] and then I wouldn't be able to continue this affair. He was concerned that I would fall out of this dissociative state and I wouldn't need him anymore. He believed that I was using him to satisfy my unhappiness in my marriage. So he was right in a lot of ways.

When did it turn scary?

We were in my car and he threatened to physically hurt me. He leaned over—I was in the driver's seat—and he put his hands around my throat and said, "I'm going to choke you." And then he took my purse and threw it out the window. People were walking by. There was a woman looking. And then he just got out of the car.

Was that the beginning of the end?

Yeah. I had to take out a restraining order.

Did he ever threaten to tell your husband or the people you worked with?

Yes. There was blackmail. We had spent the night in a hotel room and I learned that he took pictures of me while I was sleeping.

Naked pictures?

Yeah. After I told him it was over, he developed them, printed them out, and brought them to the shelter. And he got another social worker to help him write a letter to the board to make sure that I would never be a social worker again. He was smart in that way. If he couldn't have me as something to control then he would destroy my life. And now he had evidence. A couple weeks later, somehow he managed to get my father's name and he left a *very* detailed message on his voice mail at work. He also sent him a letter. And he sent another copy to my house. I was there the day it came. My husband opened it. And it was *nasty*.

Can you remember anything that it said?

"I fucked your wife here and there and on the couch and everywhere."

Was Voldemort open to reconciling after all this came out?

Some days he would say that he was but I knew that there wasn't going to be any reconciling. He was so angry—and understandably so. But I think it gave him an excuse not to ever take any responsibility for his part in the failed marriage. Even two years later, we were sitting in a synagogue, it was Yom Kippur, and he came up to me and told me that he forgave me. And I said, "I forgive you, too." And he just looked at me, like, "Forgive *me*? For *what*?"

He wouldn't own any of it?

Nothing.

What's the most important lesson you've learned from all of this?

I was not living an honest life. Even before I broke all the rules, I wasn't living an honest life because I wasn't facing the fact that this was not a marriage I should be in. I was just living this huge lie—and how long can you do that for? It also taught me that nobody is exempt from fucking up really badly. And if you think you are then you're going to get into trouble.

Do you feel jaded about marriage or are you optimistic about the future?

I am whole now, looking for a partner. And I feel so grateful for what I know I will have the next time.

What?

True love.

"If monogamy feels like a sacrifice then you're not with the right person."

ALIAS: Rachel

OCCUPATION: Consultant

YEAR OF BIRTH: 1949

CURRENT MARRIAGE STATUS: Married

DO YOU HAVE ANY CHILDREN? Yes. Two. Ages thirty-two and thirty-five

WHERE YOU GREW UP: Massachusetts

WHERE YOU LIVE: Pennsylvania

YEAR OF MARRIAGE: 1967, 1992

HOW LONG YOU DATED BEFORE YOU WERE MARRIED: Two years,
   four years

YEAR OF DIVORCE: 1991

You've been happily married to your second husband for twenty years now. What did you learn about romance from your divorce?

I once got my current husband a card—on the outside it said, "You spoil me," and on the inside it said, "I like that in a person." I think romance has to do with spoiling each other—cherishing them and making them feel special. It doesn't take a lot of flowers and diamonds to do that. It's much more about attitude. But more than anything else, I think a healthy marriage demands respect.

Is it dangerous to believe in fairy tales?

Yes, I do think there is a danger in being too romantic and believing in fairy tales. A perfect example is my sister-in-law, who so passionately believes in love that she's been married four times.

Can anybody ever really complete anybody else?

In *The Prophet,* Kahlil Gibran talks about marriage and says, "Let there be spaces in your togetherness." I know that, for me, those spaces are often where I find my sense of self.

How do you cultivate that separateness without drifting too far apart?
I think in a healthy marriage the "couple" is a third party in the relationship. Each person needs to keep their own self alive and nurtured in order for the couple to survive. That was what I missed in my first marriage—loving and knowing myself. I did not feel completed; I felt suffocated.

Is monogamy an active choice or a passive sacrifice?
If monogamy feels like a sacrifice then you're not with the right person.

People who have been divorced have a higher chance of getting divorced again. Have you seen that pattern among your friends?
No, most of my happily married friends are with their second spouse.

Why do you think that is?
Do you know that George Bernard Shaw quote?

I don't.
He defined second marriage as "the triumph of hope over experience."

Oh, I like that.
I do, too.

"A man falls in love with a woman hoping she won't change—and she does. And a woman falls in love with a man hoping he *will* change—and he doesn't."

ALIAS: Ingrid

OCCUPATION: Between jobs

YEAR OF BIRTH: 1978

CURRENT MARRIAGE STATUS: Separated, divorce pending

DO YOU HAVE ANY CHILDREN? No

WHERE YOU GREW UP: Minnesota

WHERE YOU LIVE: California

YEAR OF MARRIAGE: 2004

HOW LONG YOU DATED BEFORE YOU WERE MARRIED: Exactly one
   year—we got married on the one-year anniversary of our getting together

Yes, I thought I could change Martin. He's one of those doomed poet types—handsome, cynical, clever, moody. And it's all very exciting, and the fights are dramatic, and you really feel like you're the one that's going to finally make them settle down. He was just that stereotype of a guy, one of those people who's so disgustingly talented that you just want to throw your hands up. He came from a very privileged upbringing, draws amazingly well, can pick up a guitar and basically play anything. But he doesn't have the guts to even go to the occasional open mic night. He will do nothing with all that talent because he's that freaked out about judgment or failing.

I was not the little girl who dreamt about her wedding day. It wasn't like, *I have to get married by the time I'm twenty-five, thirty.* . . . But literally, the first time I saw Martin, the first thought that went through my head was, "I want to marry him."

I was living in London. I had just gotten out of a three-year relationship with a stable guy. I always bounced from Doomed Poet to Stable Guy. Could not handle Stable Guy. Needed to get out, climbing the walls. Cheated on Stable Guy. Then I met Martin. Martin's always the guy where *he's* the catch. Because you can't pin him down—but you want to.

I knew that he had a problem with alcoholism because I knew his ex-girlfriend. But you don't notice that people are alcoholics when you first meet them because you're just going out and getting drunk anyway, and it's fun. But then I started noticing that he would get *really* drunk and get nasty and leave me in bars. I remember once, like three or four months into our relationship, we were at a party and he was so drunk and he kissed some girl right in front of me. And I was like, "Martin, you can't do that!" And he was like, "But I was so drunk and we were so good that I thought I could kiss that girl, and then you could kiss her, and everything would be fine." I had to literally carry him out. Then he laid down on the train tracks and I had to get him off before the train came. That was our first fight where I was like, "Oh, my God, this is really scary."

But then he comes back the next day, profusely apologetic: "I'll never do that again, I don't want to lose you, I'm so sorry, I'll change." And you just accept it. Then it's this cyclical thing. It would happen occasionally before we got married but I just put on blinders.

What I didn't realize until later was—Martin is the person who *always* has to be at the party until six in the morning. And I just couldn't keep up with him. I think he thought that I was this rock 'n' roll party girl and then all of a sudden I wasn't. Like I had flipped on my end of the bargain. Because when you're falling in love, you *do* stay at the party until six in the morning. And that's what I think is so interesting. That a man falls in love with a woman hoping she won't change—and she does. And a woman falls in love with a man hoping he *will* change—and he doesn't. So yeah, I do feel like I pulled a bait and switch on him because I wasn't the girl he thought I was.

*   *   *

52

Things didn't really deteriorate, they happened very suddenly. This was maybe a year and nine months into our marriage, just before our two-year anniversary. We'd had an ugly fight. We got back to the apartment, it was late, and he was like, "I can't do this anymore—I'm leaving." And he walked out. He disappeared. I was up all night, really trying to understand what he was going through. "Okay, he's a commitment-phobe, we'll get him through this, he just needs more space."

The next morning, I'm crying getting ready for work. I'm crying in the shower. I walk to work, I'm crying on the street. I get into work and my friend is like, "You cannot stay here in this state." So she pulls me out to a coffee shop. I'm crying in the coffee shop. I was a zombie. Five days later, I come home and Martin's waiting in our apartment. "I made a mistake, I'm so stupid." But I decided to play the mature person and I said, "If we get back together now, things will just get to a head in six months. Why don't you try living alone in a studio apartment and see if you miss our life together. Then we'll figure it out."

So he leaves. This was October, November. In December, we had tickets to go see my family in Maryland for Christmas. We hadn't really seen each other in three months and we decided that Christmas would be a fresh start. So we get to the airport . . . and his passport isn't valid to go to the United States. It was surreal. I get on the flight, I'm freaking out. Martin stays in London.

When I got back, we were walking on eggshells with each other, living in the apartment together. Then one night he called me up at work: "I feel like going out. Do you want to meet at a club?" I was excited, he seemed in good spirits. We went out, we were having a good night, and then at two in the morning he's like, "I have this friend, this coworker, she's just been laid off, her father just died, she's been drinking a lot—I think I have to go take care of her." So I said, "Okay, I know what it's like to have friends go through shit—go be with your friend."

He asked me to take his bag home, so I did. And I swear to

God, this sounds so . . . well, I was looking in his bag for a Xanax and I came across his journal. And I saw all this stuff about some girl named Lara. *I love Lara, Lara's great. Should I be throwing all this away, what I already have?*

So I called up my friend: "I think Martin's been cheating on me. I found his journal and he's talking about this girl named Lara. And in the back of the journal there's the initials L.B. with a phone number. I think I have Lara's phone number." And she was like, "Call her!"

So I called her and it went to voice mail. I called again—like, five times—and it just kept going to voice mail. Then I called Martin and his phone was turned off. Finally, the sixth time I called her, I left this message: "Hi, Lara, I'm Martin's wife. I think maybe you're with him right now, I'm not sure, but if you could call me back it'd be great."

I was calm. I wasn't crying. I had never—not once in three months of all this bullshit back and forth—ever thought there was another girl. So finally, ten minutes go by, and Martin called: "Lara just received this really weird message from you. What are you talking about?"

And I was like, "Oh, okay, so that's Lara, the girl you're cheating on me with?"

"What are you talking about?"

"You're cheating on me with that girl."

"No, I told you, we're friends."

And I was like, "Martin, I found your journal."

"I don't keep a journal."

"No? I *have* the journal—*in my hands*. It's a leather-bound journal."

"I don't have a journal."

And I was like, "*Martin* . . . Do you want me to *read you passages from your journal?*"

"Yes, read me passages."

So there I was, on the phone, reading him passages about this girl named Lara. Finally, he's like, "Okay, stop, enough. I don't want to hear it anymore. What do you want me to do?"

"I want you to come home."

So he came home and he was still in complete denial. And I was just like, "This explains the entire three months—you should have just told me!"

I ended up taking my stuff and moving out that night. I was so angry, I didn't want to talk to him, didn't want to deal with him. However, I did do some sketchy things. I broke into his e-mail and I saw some really horrible chats between the two of them where he was like, "I couldn't get on that plane [to Maryland]." Like he just couldn't *tear himself away from her*. And I'm like, *Bullshit*! You couldn't get on that plane because your passport was invalid! And there was all this other stuff: *I'm with her but I'm thinking about you*. And really intimate sexual stuff that I did not want to know about. Just *awful*.

I was staying with a friend at this point. A week later, Martin called me up at work: "I need you to come to lunch with me, anywhere you want, I'll be there." So I came to lunch and he's like, "I've been thinking about this Lara thing. It was a stupid, passing infatuation—you're the one I want to be with. I'm going to completely cut her out of my life. Take some time off of work—let's go to Paris. I'll book the tickets and we'll work it all out. We'll start from scratch."

Paris is where we went on our honeymoon. So I thought about it and I was like, "Okay, that makes sense. Let's get out of London, let's go to Paris." I get back from the lunch and I'm elated. I'm on a cloud. I'm like, "He made his decision, fuck that girl, it was stupid—I'm totally willing to forgive."

Now, I had actually planned on sleeping out that night. I had an Italian class and then I was seeing a good friend of mine for sushi and I was going to sleep at her house. And I don't know why I did this, but I blew off Italian class and I blew off sushi with my friend. I just wanted to go home. And that's what changed everything. Because Martin did not expect me there. That's what haunts me.

I got back at five o'clock. I walked into the apartment and there was blood everywhere . . . blood in the kitchen . . . blood along the hall. And we had a cat, so there were all these bloody paw prints all over the floor. And I found Martin in the bathtub, having slit his wrists.

My first thought was, "He's dead. I came home to a dead man." No question about it, he's blue, he's not breathing. I called the police and, I remember, my first words were: "He's dead. You have to come but I think he's dead."

Meanwhile, his phone was ringing off the hook. I looked to see who it was—and it's Lara. *It's the girl.* So I answered his phone and I was like, "Lara, you've got to come here now, I think he's dying." So Lara jumped into a cab and raced over. And I realized in retrospect: *She has our door code!* So we hugged each other and we both got into an ambulance with Martin on the way to the hospital.

After, we went to a bar around the corner and got blind drunk together and exchanged stories. She's like, "Martin told me you were in the process of being separated but that you didn't know anybody here and so he had to be protective of you because you were this fragile little American in London." And I was like, "No, we were never really broken up, he was making attempt after attempt to get back together with me." Meanwhile, her jaw was dropping. My jaw was dropping. And we looked eerily similar, like carbon copies of each other. It was *creepy.* She's like, "Why would he cheat on you with me? We look alike!"

We closed down four bars. And when we got back to the hospital the next morning, we were like, "Yeah, we've been drinking all night, we actually really like each other. You, on the other hand . . ."

*   *   *

The first time I ever talked about all this it was very hard, but I'm okay with admitting it now. Harder than anything is the moment where you realize that part of you wishes he hadn't made it. In spite of yourself, you're like, *I just wish he would have died*. And people tell you, "Yeah, you think that until you're planning the funeral and then you'd never wish that." But at the time, part of me just wished I hadn't found him. Because being a widow's easier than being a divorcée.

Martin's doing okay now. He spent about two months in the hospital. And he was trying to get Lara back. He was playing both of us, but she was buying it. She was doing the nursemaid thing that I used to do. So many girls like playing nursemaid to men. She was going to save him, like *I* was going to save him, the way his *past* girlfriend was going to save him. You fall prey to it until you wise up.

I want a stable guy now. I don't want any more starving artists. No more doomed poets! It's funny, I have friends nowadays who are thinking of their partners in terms of *He would make an awesome ex-husband. We could get married, have kids, split up, and I know it would be amicable. I know I could deal with him on a day-to-day basis as the father of my children but not as my partner.*

There's this article I read about how we're supposed to have three partners in our life. The person that opens us up sexually—the mentor figure when we're younger. Then the father of our children. Then, once the children have grown up and left the home, the marriage of true minds, which I'm seeing more and more of.

Like with my parents. They got divorced when I was twenty years old. My father was Mr. Irresponsibility—the fun-loving, freewheeling hippie who eventually had to settle down and get a job and insurance because he had three kids to support. And he was *miserable*. But now he's completely different because he's with a woman who suits him. She's a total hippie, too. They don't care what their house looks like, they smoke pot and go on camping trips and kayak together. They're *perfect* for each other. And my mother is now married to a person she went on a date with when she was fourteen years old. He found her forty years later through an alumni network. So they're embarking on this whole new relationship and that's probably who she'll die with.

And it's funny because my mom totally loved Martin and she still has this loyalty to him, like, "Oh, if only he could get his act together." But I realized—you have to stop with the "ifs" and the "buts." Because if Martin could get his act together, Martin wouldn't be Martin. He'd be a different person. And yet still, to this day, even after all that happened, she'll say something like, "I just wish the two of you could work it out."

And I'm just like, *Mommmmmm*.

"We were very much alike, we were both extremely independent, but looking back, we allowed too much water to go under the bridge. We allowed *too much* independence."

ALIAS: Andro

OCCUPATION: Cinematographer

YEAR OF BIRTH: 1971

CURRENT MARRIAGE STATUS: Married

DO YOU HAVE ANY CHILDREN? Yes, a daughter with my second wife

WHERE YOU GREW UP: Eastern Europe and Boston

WHERE YOU LIVE: Austin, Texas

YEAR OF MARRIAGE: 1999, 2007

HOW LONG YOU DATED BEFORE YOU WERE MARRIED: Four years,
     nine months

YEAR OF DIVORCE: 2003

I ran away from home when I was sixteen and traveled around the world for about ten years until I met Eva, which kind of put a stop to my traveling. I'd just been through the craziest story with this woman who I met in Italy. I was really into her. She told me she was twenty-nine years old but I found out that she was actually thirty-six and that she'd just broken up with a guy who was connected to the mob and who was extremely jealous. She broke up with him because he couldn't get her pregnant. And one night she confessed to me that she wasn't on birth control and that she wanted me to get her pregnant. She said that if I wanted to stick around I would be taken care of because her family was very wealthy, and if not, she would raise the child herself.

At first I was like, "All right, that seems fine." Because I felt some empathy for her situation. But the next morning I woke up and I was like, "What the fuck am I doing?" So I bailed and went to an island off the coast of France, where I got a job as a waiter at this *crêperie*. There was no English spoken on this island, it was very authentic, and one of the guys at the restaurant told me that there was an American girl who worked as a cocktail waitress at a local bar. So we went there one night and I met her.

She was four years older than me; I was extremely attracted to her. She was mixed-race. High cheekbones. Stunning. Very strong and funny and just very passionate. There was a little flirtation but it didn't seem like it was going anywhere because she had a boyfriend who was away for the summer. So we were friends at first. The relationship took a month to progress, and then after we started seeing each other, her boyfriend showed up. I remember her behaving very coldly to him. Then he approached me and wanted to speak; you could see the guy was upset. I said, "There's nothing we have to say to each other. This is between you and Eva."

But I remember it created a feeling in me very early on, like, if she'd done this to him, she could potentially do the same thing to me.

Eva is from Oklahoma and she had a monstrous childhood. She had a Mexican father and an American Indian mother and they were alcoholics and drug addicts. When she was three years old, her mother left her under the bed and she was bit by a rat that had rabies and they had to rush her to the hospital. So the state took her away and put her with a foster family.

I'm trying not to go into this too much because if I talk about it, I start crying, and I don't want to go to that place. But, like, her toes went across like this [in a straight line] because her foster parents wouldn't buy her new shoes, so her feet didn't grow properly. And her sister's head—she was also adopted—was flat on the back because you can't leave a child in a crib, and they would leave her in the crib all the time.

So all these things were present. Every time I'd look at her feet it would make me think about what she'd gone through. I really felt like I was caring for someone who was wounded, someone who hadn't been given the opportunity to be loved. I remember waking up in the middle of the night when she was sleeping and caressing her back or her head and just feeling so much empathy and love for her. And she never used any of it as an excuse—she would just talk about it like "it happened" as opposed to it being this thing that defined her.

She'd been living in France for years, spoke perfectly, no accent, and we got along extremely well because she was very passionate about art and film and culture. She broke up with that boyfriend, and when the summer ended on the island, we decided to move to Aix-en-Provence in the South of France. I couldn't find a job, I didn't have a work permit anymore. But that was the most amazing part of our relationship, when we were struggling to make it, when it was us against the world. Nothing fazed us.

Around that time, Eva applied to AFI—the American Film Institute—and was accepted. That was her dream. I said, "All right, we'll go stay at my mother's house in Boston, make some money, buy a car, drive to LA, and you can start school in September."

So we went to Boston and then drove to LA. And after one week I said, "Look, I love you, but I can't live in this city."

And she was like, "But I really want to go to AFI."

And I was like, "Well, I can't stay here."

I knew that she wouldn't stay without me, so I was conflicted. But I was twenty-five years old and selfish. I still have guilt that I didn't support her. Unfortunately, at that age, I didn't know how to compromise for another person. So she gave up her dream and we moved to San Francisco. It was the beginning of the whole dot-com era and I somehow managed to get a job at a small ad agency.

All of a sudden, we had some money. We got a nice apartment in Pacific Heights. But the better I did financially, the more complacent I felt, and the more I knew this wasn't the life I wanted to be living. I was already talking about having kids, but whenever we'd talk about it, she was always pushing it off, saying, "In three years . . . in two years . . . after we're married."

Everybody would always say how much they admired our relationship, how independent we were. I was traveling a lot, I'd be gone for months at a time, and she started having these friendships with guys that I didn't know, which brought out insecurities in me that I didn't know I had. I felt jealous in ways that I'd never felt before. And I told her, "This makes me uncomfortable"—which put her on the defensive. I was just saying that we should all hang out together so that I understand the dynamic and feel good about it. But that didn't go over well because she thought I was trying to control her.

I remember one time, before we were married, we went to Boston to visit my family for Thanksgiving and she was really distant the whole night. We went out to a bar and she asked one of my friends where she could get some coke. And at the end of the night, she was gone. I found her in the bathroom hooking up with a woman. They were making out or something. And I was really hurt by that and we had a big fight. Again, it was that whole thing: "You're not going to control me."

I decided to propose, thinking that we would stop living such independent lives and come together to start a family. We got married in France on the same island where we met, and everybody who went said it was one of the most incredible weddings they'd ever been to. It was this weeklong party and we all stayed in this château and everybody cooked and drank. But there was this distance in her. For the first time, she didn't want to be intimate. Twice in a month we had sex. That had never been an issue before.

When we got back to San Francisco, things were good for about five or six months, and then they really started to deteriorate. We'd been together for eight years, and for the first time she would do things where I would just start to think, "I can't stand to be around her anymore."

She was really hardheaded and opinionated, so she would piss a lot of people off. Because of where she came from, she had built this new identity for herself as this independent French woman. But this was San Francisco in the nineties, most of the people we were hanging out with weren't artists, they were advertising people. We'd go to a friend's house and if it was decorated like a frat boy, she would make fun of him. Or if we'd go to a dinner and somebody would say something ignorant, she would say something about it. I actually loved it in the beginning, but after a while it just got tiring. And the more she drank, the more it happened. She'd always say it with a laugh, but she had fun jabbing at people—she didn't care about what effect it had.

One of our biggest fights was when I said that I wanted to quit smoking, but she kept smoking in the apartment. I got really angry: "How can you not support me wanting to quit?" And she was like, "You're not going to tell me what I can and can't do!" She was really pissed. She would not go outside to smoke.

It's such a cliché—everybody says it's a compromise—but it really is. We were very much alike, we were both extremely independent, but looking back, we allowed too much water to go under the bridge. We allowed *too much* independence. And we had fundamentally different ideas about what it meant to be a family. For a long time, I just accepted everything because of the upbringing she had. Even though she never used it as an excuse, I kind of did. But when she said, "I don't want to have children anymore," that's when things really started to deteriorate.

My upbringing was such that I wanted to have a huge family, but she just had no model for that. And that really was the basis for the split. Ultimately, we just had conflicting wants, and we became frustrated. And then we started to not like certain things about each other. And then that started to create space and distance. And then that turned into resentment. And then that space and distance and resentment wound up ending the relationship.

I never thought I would get married again and I never thought I was going to have children. Then, one night, I was traveling through LA and I met Allison. I was supposed to move back to Europe, but I postponed my trip so we could go out on a date. We moved in with each other a month later and got married eight months after that. We have a four-year-old daughter.

Had I met Allison when I was in my twenties, I don't think the relationship would have worked because I wasn't mature enough to know how to treat her respectfully. Not "respectfully" in the way of opening doors—I'm talking about being aware of her feelings and emotions and not doing things that would make her feel vulnerable or insecure or second to myself. I never did that with Eva. I'm much less selfish now, much less self-centered. With Allison, if she said, "I want to go to AFI," I would stay in LA.

"It's easy to romanticize things and to see your spouse how you want them to be rather than how they really are."

ALIAS: Carolyn

OCCUPATION: Decorator

YEAR OF BIRTH: 1979

CURRENT MARRIAGE STATUS: Divorced

DO YOU HAVE ANY CHILDREN? Yes, an eight-year-old son with my ex-
husband

WHERE YOU GREW UP: Michigan

WHERE YOU LIVE: New York

YEAR OF MARRIAGE: 2000

HOW LONG YOU DATED BEFORE YOU WERE MARRIED: One and a
half years

YEAR OF DIVORCE: 2008

My parents are born-again Christians. They believe in marriage until death. I was raised with religion as a central part of my life: church on Sunday, youth group on Thursday, weeklong church retreats, church camps in the summer—even church camps in the *winter*. But I was a rebellious kid, I tested everything and got into a lot of trouble. I remember once secretly going to Planned Parenthood in high school to get tested for HIV because I had had oral sex and didn't know if I could get a disease! I'd been taught my whole life that you grow up and do that *marriage* thing. That's what you're supposed to do, and so that's what I did.

At first I felt very codependent and reliant on David, my ex. I was twenty-one and a new mother at twenty-two, trying to finish college, and we lived several states away from any relatives. It's easy to romanticize things and to see your spouse how you want them to be rather than how they really are. I remember hearing this amazing story about how he liked this girl and he made a trail of pennies all the way from her doorstep down the block leading to something, I don't remember what. And I thought that was so sweet! I longed for him to be that way in our relationship, but he was very rarely romantic with me.

I always think about the time he bought me a mirror for my birthday the first year we were married. This small, round, shitty mirror. I didn't need a mirror and I couldn't figure out what the hell he was trying to say to me. I always held on to this ideal of the penny story, and maybe I set myself up for being unhappy. But maybe it's also hard to romance a woman who doesn't want to fuck you.

Looking back, David was the first guy who ever paid attention to me during sex. He was the first guy that ever made me orgasm. So this was very confusing when I was twenty. It was the best I'd ever had in the bedroom. But once we were married, we rarely had sex—even though he wanted it regularly. And this became a horrible issue: me feeling guilty and grossed out by sex, and him feeling rejected and unsatisfied and pent up. And I really tried! I went to sex therapy, I bought all these books, I brought home toys from Babeland. But it got to the point where I'd just do it so we wouldn't have an argument. And I felt sick inside. He never forced me or anything, but there was this sort of entitlement. It made me very angry that he could want to have sex and be so intimate but have no consideration or awareness of what I was feeling.

I remember telling David when we were dating that I was attracted to women and that I didn't know what that was all about. But we were twenty, and you say a lot when you're twenty, so I don't think he put much stock in it. Years later, I did meet a gay lady and we became good friends, never beyond, and that definitely was a part of what initiated things. I remember going to Catty Shack, this big lesbian bar in Park Slope, to watch *The L Word* and absolutely loving it. Finally, I just realized that all my sexual fantasies were about women. It took me eight years to fully accept and realize that I was gay and wanted to fuck and be with women. Eight years of me trying to love David but not being able to be a lover. I don't know how I did it for so long, and I especially don't know how David did it.

I remember telling him while he was doing the dishes—it just came out. I felt so relieved and afraid. He was very calm, I'm sure he knew. And we talked about it. I told him he should have an affair—that I seriously didn't want to know about it, but I was fine with it. But he is exceptionally loyal and has deep-rooted morals and he dismissed my go-ahead. I also think he has a martyr or a victim nature.

Finally, we decided I should go to therapy and figure it all out. Being raised so Christian, well, they instill a lot of beliefs in you. Divorce just seems very much like a failure, and there is something sneering about it: *You couldn't make it work?* There was talk here and there, like maybe we can make some sort of arrangement, but that was all bullshit.

I had to tell my folks over the phone, since they live in Michigan. Just thinking about it made me queasy. Not only was I getting a divorce—which is a sin—but I was gay! My mom said that if I robbed a bank, she would not hate me, the sinner, but hate the sin. I'm not sure how being gay is like robbing a bank, but that's the analogy she used. She started blaming herself, thinking she had not been a good and proper mother and that's how I "turned gay." I remember my dad angrily saying, "Why did you have to go and do *that*?" I guess they just couldn't believe that their God could ever make someone gay. It challenges what is black and white for them, so they have to believe it's some sort of psychological disorder. Now, almost two years after coming out, they seem to be okay with it.

I was first with a woman about four months after David moved out. I had struck up a friendship with a woman named Ellie, which naturally progressed into the relationship I am still in today. I took it slow, but when we did finally have sex, there was all the awkwardness of being with someone for the first time, but it was this feeling of "finally!"

I never really thought sex was such a big deal; it just caused pain between people. What was so remarkable was how my body reacted, and was so stimulated, and sexual, and just absolutely craved to fuck and be fucked. I had never felt that reaction before—I guess I just never felt turned on or sexual with a man. And my God, just admiring her body. The *sweat,* the *smell.* I couldn't get enough of the smell! And hands are amazing, amazing things. Hands can move in ways that penetration with a man just can't. And it almost always culminates with a climax. Hetero couples should definitely take much more advantage of their hands.

"If you're having this amazing sex with somebody, you think, 'Oh, it's love! This person's so amazing and they're so loving when we're having sex.' It becomes like a drug. But oftentimes, the truth is: They just love sex!"

ALIAS: Olivia

OCCUPATION: Manufacturing

YEAR OF BIRTH: 1951

CURRENT MARRIAGE STATUS: Divorced

DO YOU HAVE ANY CHILDREN? Two boys and a girl

WHERE YOU GREW UP: Florida

WHERE YOU LIVE: New Mexico

YEAR OF MARRIAGE: 1977

HOW LONG YOU DATED BEFORE YOU WERE MARRIED: One month

YEAR OF DIVORCE: 1989

How did a Jewish girl from Florida wind up living on an ashram in 1975?
The baby boom generation, we were the seekers, we were the spiritualists, we were the hippies. We became passionate about gurus, meditation, self-help teachers, and many of us were part of communes where everyone lived together and shared everything. Not our husbands and wives, but the raising of the children, the making of the food. And many of us had teachers or gurus from India. Muktananda, known as "Baba," was one of the biggest and most well known. I met him in 1974.

How does one meet a guru?
One night my brother's friend insisted that I come with him to this meditation program, and as I was sitting there in that room I started to feel this incredible energy—this sense of absolute joy. It was so overpowering I just started crying. And I realized it was coming from him.

From Baba?
Yeah. He was just totally plugged into the source. He wore sunglasses because his eyes were too much—they'd knock people out.

Can you describe what that incredible energy feels like?
Love. That's really what we were all seeking: self-love. And I realized that day that I wanted more of that. So I packed up my stuff and I moved to Berkeley and started living at the ashram. And that's where I met Daniel. He would serve ice cream in this little snack shop at the ashram and I kept seeing him there and he was super handsome and sweet and just adorable. And one day I said, "Can I have a java chip ice cream with two spoons? And I'd like you to share it with me." And that was it.

What made you think that was it?
I just knew. The energy was so strong—it was so much stronger than we were. In retrospect, of course, that's not necessarily true love. It's infatuation. Infatuation can look a lot like love. I've been fooled a few times in my life.

How can you tell the difference between infatuation and love?
Time. That is the only way to see all sides of who someone is. You really have to see them when the chips are down. And you just can't do that in three months or six months or even in a year.

How long after sharing the java chip did Daniel propose?
A few weeks. At the ashram, every night there's this thing called *darshan,* which is basically being in the divine presence of someone who is enlightened. You'd pay homage to the guru, to Baba, and you'd bring food or flowers and you'd get to be close to him and ask him questions. So we were standing in line and Daniel looked really freaked out and I was like, "What's going on?" And he said, "I'm going to ask Baba if he'll marry us."

How did you react to that?

I started freaking out, too! I was thinking, "If Baba says no then it's not supposed to happen. He can't possibly say yes." But when Daniel asked, Baba started jumping around and laughing and saying, "Yes! Yes! Yes!" And he took the peacock feathers and started beating us over the head, yelling, "This is destiny!" We got married two weeks after that. It was an Indian wedding with seventeen other couples and saris and bindis on our heads. It was unbelievable.

Looking back, do you think it's unrealistic to promise to love someone unconditionally "'til death do you part"?

You can't possibly say that. I think the whole vow thing needs to be rewritten. It should be about *intention*. You can say, "I love you completely and I'm making this commitment to work on it so our love can grow." But you can't say that love is eternal—that you'll love someone forever—because you just don't know that. I don't think that romantic love between two adults, even in the healthiest sense, can be unconditional.

Do you think that we airbrush our flaws in the beginning of a relationship in an attempt to become the other person's ideal?

Oh, a tremendous amount.

How did you do that?

Well, for me, I was hearing all these things that Daniel loved about me so that's what I wanted to continue to show. I wanted to live up to it. I wanted that acceptance. And I felt like if I showed other parts of me he might not love me anymore. It's human nature. We want to be seen as having it all together.

Do you think we overprioritize passion?

Yes. You just can't maintain it in the way it was in the beginning. That's impossible. I mean, I've had great sex. But it's ultimately more about the intimacy of loving and touching and snuggling. That's what sustains. The sex thing comes and goes. It's not the most important thing. It's not the *second* most important thing. It's just a thing in the relationship that you have to have but that's not what ultimately keeps you together.

What keeps you together, romantically?
It's what I call "couch love." When you're hanging on the couch, watching TV, and the person is still rubbing your feet, massaging your back, stroking your hair just naturally because they love you. And it has to be reciprocal.

A woman I interviewed said, "Whenever you're living in passion, you're living in the fear that you're going to lose something. And if you live in that fear all the time, you're not acting out of your heart." Do you think great sex can cause delusion?
Yes. I think sex is the biggest problem with relationships. Well, it's not the *biggest* problem, but it's definitely a veil. If you're having this amazing sex with somebody, you think, "Oh, it's love! This person's so amazing and they're so loving when we're having sex." It becomes like a drug. But oftentimes, the truth is: They just love sex!

When did the veils start to lift in your marriage with Daniel?
After a couple months he said to me, "I love you but I really want to be a renunciate. I want to be a swami." That's where you renounce everything worldly and become a monk. I was sitting on the bed and he told me this and I kind of went into shock. I said, "You can't love me and feel that way." And he said, "I can and that's how I feel." And I said, "You should have thought of that before we got married." And he said, "But that's what I really want." And I said, "Well, that's not what I want," and I punched him in the shoulder and pushed him off the bed.

Was that a big turning point in the relationship?
Yes. Something changed for us and it never got healed. We stayed together for twelve years after that and for that whole time he made it very clear that being a lover of God and meditating for multiple hours a day was going to be his first priority. I came second. He told me that all the time. And I just took that as a total rejection. I was devastated because there were parts of him that I loved so much but I was constantly hurt by the parts of him that were disinterested in me.

Were you able to express those feelings of rejection?
Absolutely not. I didn't want him to think I was needy. I wanted to be the strong woman. That's what you do until you learn not to. It took me fifty-six years to realize that you have to be real, no matter how screwed up you look, otherwise you're living a lie. You're not being your authentic self. It's scary but you have to do it.

But what about compromise?
Compromise is necessary. It's really about acknowledging that we're different, accepting the differences, and then starting to love those differences.

A woman I interviewed said, "You don't want to compromise yourself into oblivion." How do you prevent that from happening?
If you're in touch with who you are and someone's asking you to compromise too much, you're going to feel it. But the thing is: Men and women are *so different*. I can't expect a man to be a chick. And I think a lot of women expect men to have the same level of sensitivity as they do.

Is that the key difference? Men are less sensitive?
I don't think men are less sensitive. I think women are sensi-

tive *more often*. That's the difference. I don't think men feel safe enough to articulate it.

Do women want the strong, silent type?
We do want the strong type but not the silent type. The silent man is the man who disappears. I think men have a real tendency to do that. They check out. And no woman wants that.

Sometimes we're not disappearing, we just need a little space.
Right, which was something I was never able to do. I think a lot of women have trouble giving a man space. And men *need* space. Because if you give them space, they will come back. They'll reconnect again and say, "Here I am. I don't know where I went or why I went there but I'm back." And that's it. You really can't change it. People evolve and grow but we don't really change who we are.

DISCUSSING THE DIRTY

———

Have I shocked you by the dirty things I wrote to you?
You think perhaps that my love is a filthy thing.
It is, darling, at some moments.
—JAMES JOYCE, from a letter
to his future wife, NORA BARNACLE

Don't tell me the moon is shining;
show me the glint of light on broken glass.
—ANTON CHEKHOV

Life is short. Have an affair.
—The slogan for ASHLEY MADISON,
an online dating site for married people
who are looking for extramarital sex.
The site claims to have more than
ten million members.

A few years ago, a friend of mine placed an ad on Craigslist for a housekeeper. He had just ended a two-year relationship with his live-in girlfriend. He was thirty-five and stoic; she was thirty and chatty. She wanted to get married; he didn't. She was hoping that he'd say something to make her stay, but he couldn't. Instead, he helped her pack and watched her go.

"It was sad," he said. "I'm *still* sad. But it was the only thing to do. She wants to get married, she should go find her husband." When people asked who broke up with whom, they both said it was mutual.

They were a good couple, fun to be around, but very old-fashioned in the gender department. He wore the pants; she wore the apron. When she moved out, the place went to seed. So he went to the store and bought a closet's worth of cleaning supplies. He came home and dumped everything in the middle of the kitchen floor. He stared at it, sizing it up, like a boxer before a bout. This went on for about a week. Then he placed the ad:

CLEANING, LADY?
My girlfriend and I just broke up and I have no idea how to clean my apartment. I was going to hire a housekeeper but I figured it would be more fun to try this first. So here goes: I'm looking for somebody to come over and clean. Either naked or in your bra and panties. My apartment is 900 square feet. I have all the proper supplies. Please send a picture if you're interested. I am a totally

normal person and this is 100% for real. I'm just kind of bored today. And I guess a little bit lonely.

Within the hour, he got six responses with no picture, two responses with pictures of women he didn't want to see naked, and one response from a woman calling herself Vivian.
She wrote:

Oh, this is perfect. I'm your girl! I'm 27, 5'7", curvy but slim in the waist, not fat, college-educated (freelance editor), and a really hard worker. I enjoy scrubbing and polishing things; have a very tidy apt myself ;) And you sound so fun just for suggesting it! Where are you located? If not too far, I'll do it for $100 and some good scotch.

They e-mailed a bit and swapped pictures, each silently wondering if the other was a psychopath. Eventually they spoke on the phone. My friend said, "I'm not a psychopath." She laughed and said, "I'm not a psychopath, either." Feeling sufficiently at ease, they made plans for her to come over at four-thirty that afternoon.

She arrived on time wearing a long coat. He greeted her at the door and invited her in. She entered his apartment and looked around. Then she stripped—no tease, all business. Wearing sneakers, socks, a black bra, and underwear, she gestured to the scotch. My friend poured two shots from a brand-new bottle of Lagavulin. They clinked glasses and drank a bit. Then she asked, "What do you want me to do?"

He shrugged, pointing to the cleaning supplies: "That's why you're here."

She smiled as if to say, "*Is* it now?"

Then she finished her drink and picked up the Swiffer. My friend watched her as she did the dishes, dusted the blinds, and took out the trash. She got down on her hands and knees and scrubbed every inch of the bathroom, skillfully, willfully. When she finished, a few hours later, the place was immaculate, and the Lagavulin was almost gone.

She stood before him in the living room: "Will that be all?"

"Wow," he said, looking around, impressed. "Thank you."

"Thank *you*," she said. "Would you mind if I take a quick shower?"

"Not at all."

She walked toward the bathroom, aware of his eyes on her. In front of the mirror, she took off her shoes, her socks, her bra. She turned on the water but did not close the door. At this point, my friend swears on his mother's life that he called out, "Vivian, you've done so much cleaning for me, can I do any cleaning for you?"

In response to this zinger, she apparently smiled, slid off her underwear, and stepped into the shower. My friend followed. They got soapy quickly, kissing, exploring, and then she knelt down before him, the water against her back, and gave him a blow job, swallowing.

She shut off the water. They got out and dried off, as if nothing strange had just happened. She asked, "Anything else before I go?" Again, my friend swears on his mother's life that he said, "My duvet. I hate putting that cover thing on."

Without a word, she went over to the bed and started putting the cover on. My friend came up behind her. She turned; they kissed; he threw her down on the duvet. They had sex, with abandon, with a condom.

"It was *dirty*," he said, gloating.

She obviously agreed because when he offered her the $100, she accepted, saying, "Only because I cleaned. I'm not a whore; the sex was free. If you wanna do it again—the sex, I mean—call me. You have my number."

She kissed him on the lips, put on her clothes, and left without making the bed.

* * *

This story is relevant for three reasons:

1. They saw each other again, twice.
2. Both times, she called him.
3. Vivian had been married for five years.

I'm not suggesting that every wife with a boring sex life is going around acting like Catherine Deneuve in *Belle de jour*. But these interviews have convinced me that no matter how prurient our urges, they will always find an outlet—if not at home, then elsewhere. With life spans increasing as they are and most Americans remaining very conservative about open marriage, modern husbands and wives are faced with the nearly impossible task of being each other's everything in the bedroom for upward of sixty years.

So how do you hit on your spouse?

In her book *Mating in Captivity,* the therapist Esther Perel writes, "It always amazes me how much people are willing to experiment sexually outside their relationships, yet how tame and puritanical they are at home with their partners." If desire is the root of eroticism, she wonders, how can we desire what we already have?

The key, she says, is to nurture the naughty by cultivating separateness and acknowledging that our day-to-day emotional needs may be antithetical to what turns us on in the bedroom. For example, healthy relationships tend to be based on feelings of familiarity, safety, security, and equality. But sexual desire thrives on the shadier side: on mystery, risk, transgression, polarity, and taboo. In other words, democracy may work in the daylight but at night it can be fun to fuck a fascist.

"You can't go into a relationship or a marriage without discussing the dirty," says Liz. "You need to know each other's boundaries."

"I know now what it feels like when someone touches you because they *want* to and not because they're *supposed* to," says

Ann. "I think if you ever feel like an obligation or a burden then you're not in a good relationship at all."

"I became one of those guys who basically had to ask for a blow job on his birthday," says Steve.

"I know that I'm seen by many as this freaky kind of guy," says Paul. "I didn't want to be such a 'kinky bastard,' I really didn't."

Neither did Vivian.

During their second tryst at my friend's apartment, she confessed that she loves her husband but that she's been unhappy at home for some time. Compromise turned to sacrifice, sacrifice to rejection, rejection to resentment, and resentment to Craigslist. She didn't want a divorce, she said—she was just looking for a little escape.

In the spirit of full disclosure, my friend admitted that he'd placed the ad as a way to furnish his own fantasies in the wake of a difficult breakup. So he asked her nicely, "Can we please not talk about this stuff?"

When my friend finished telling me the story, he looked up, his eyes shifting between pride and shame.

"Inspiring," I said, offering a round of applause.

"How so?"

At the time I wasn't sure, but that question was in the back of my mind as I spoke to hundreds of people about their most deviant desires. And while I've always admired my friend's moxie, it wasn't until recently that I realized why this story had such an impact on me. It's not that I want to be the type of guy who places sex ads on Craigslist. I just want to make sure that I'm never the type of husband whose wife would want to answer one.

"You have to have that *urge*. And you *both* have to have it. You don't say, 'We're going to have sex on Monday.' *No*. He might come in from a golf match, all filthy dirty, and then all of a sudden you're in bed and you're having a hell of a time!"

ALIAS: Pauline

OCCUPATION: Retired

YEAR OF BIRTH: 1915

CURRENT MARRIAGE STATUS: Widowed

DO YOU HAVE ANY CHILDREN? Two

WHERE YOU GREW UP: New York

WHERE YOU LIVE: Arizona

YEAR OF MARRIAGE: 1923, 1941, 1959

HOW LONG YOU DATED BEFORE YOU WERE MARRIED: About a year each

YEAR OF DIVORCE: 1939, 1943

Did you have lots of boyfriends growing up in the 1930s?
I never had boyfriend trouble. I always had plenty of guys. *Always*.

You've been married three times. Tell me about the first.
Oh, Christ. The first time was right after I graduated from prep school. I was seventeen years old—what did I know about living? *Nothing*. He wasn't for me, but I married him anyway. I had my kids with him, so it was worth it. Then I divorced him. Then someone fixed me up with a man from Chattanooga. He was the cheapest son of a bitch that ever lived. So I divorced him, too.

Just for being cheap? What else didn't you like about him?
I'm telling you a very intimate thing here. [She lowers her voice.] His ding dong was very small. So he went for an operation and they made it bigger.

He splurged on that?
Yes, he did. But I couldn't stay married to him.

Why not?
He was too cheap [laughs]! Then I married Bill Simmons. He was quite a man, I'm telling you. He was terrific. Very bright. And he was *mad* about me. We had a wonderful time. But he died, and I haven't been married since. Although I did have a lover. One special man.

What was he like?
He was married [laughs]! His daughter was married to my brother, okay? He was in the ready-to-wear business. He was one of the big shots when they started making T-shirts. We went together for years. I used to meet him on Saturdays and we'd go to a suite at the Waldorf-Astoria.

So you've had three husbands and one lover. Which one were you the most mad about?
My lover.

Why?
An affair is very different than a marriage because you can break it off at any time. And this man made life very exciting. It was never dull around him. I like when a man has money and he can take me places and buy me things. All women do. Don't let anybody tell you differently, okay? If he would buy his wife a present, he would buy me a better one. He once bought her a diamond heart, and the next day he brought me a gorgeous diamond bracelet, very expensive. You see what I'm telling you? Tit for tat. Nothing was too good for me.

So we need to make our marriages more like affairs—is that your advice?

Yes. *Then* it becomes exciting!

How was his relationship with his wife?
He never got along with his wife. I shouldn't say *never*—what do I know? Her family had money, they were in the fish business. He didn't come from money, and I think that's why he married her. But he was always running around.

Did his wife know?
I'll tell you a story. They used to have a summer place up in Maine. One day, they were on their way up there and they stopped by my work—I worked in a shoe factory at the time. And *she* came into my office and said, "Would you please come with us?" And I said, "*Hell,* no. What am I going up there for?" And she said, "Because he's miserable without you." I'll never forget that.

Did you go?
Yeah, I went.

So she knew the whole time?
She knew. But she couldn't do anything about it. She was a nice lady, but she wasn't a *pretty* lady. And she wasn't an *exciting* lady. But they stayed married until he died. I'm sure he had many women in his life besides me.

Did your brother and his wife know?
Yes. Because she said to me just a short while ago, "I knew about the affair between you and my father. He was *crazy* about you."

Were you hoping that he'd leave his wife for you?
Oh, when something belongs to me, I want it. But I knew I could never marry him because my whole family would be involved.

And that wouldn't be good at all. My father, he used to say to me, "Are you happy?" And I'd say, "Yeah." And he'd say, "Good, stay that way—it's better than being *un*happy."

What else did your father teach you about love?
Listen, my father was a run-around, too. All the men from that generation who came to this country and made a few bucks, they all ran around.

How about the women?
At that time, no. Not so much. Now it's different. Now everybody runs around!

Do you think it's okay to run around?
Well, I wouldn't want my daughter to do it. If she was unhappy, I would want her to get a divorce and meet a nice guy. And she did! Her second husband is a wonderful guy. He's just mad about her. And she likes him, too. I don't know how much she *loves* him, but I know he's very good to her.

Did any of your husbands run around?
No. Well, I should say that I never *caught* any of them.

Let's talk about Bill Simmons for a second. Your third husband.
Oh, he was wonderful.

What made that marriage so good?
First of all, you have to be sexually compatible. That's very important. If anyone tells you different, they're nuts. And he was extravagant; he liked living the way I did. We used to dance, which I love to do. We used to drink, have a few cocktails. And he had a lot of friends. I met them all. They were all cheaters.

Most men are cheaters—you know that, don't you? I could meet a cheater tomorrow if I wanted to. But I've had enough men. I'm ninety-six years old. What the hell do I want a man for? What can I give him? What can he give me? *Nothing.*

What advice would you give to a couple that's been married for ten years and is looking to spice up their sex life?
First of all, a man mustn't be selfish. He's had his orgasm, he's got to make sure she's had hers, too. That whole *wham, bam, thank you, ma'am*—that's no good. But it's very hard to spice things up after ten years. If you haven't got that feeling, and he hasn't got that feeling, get a divorce. It's the only way. You're better off alone. Because when you live with someone that doesn't make you happy, it's *miserable.* It's *worse* than being alone.

Do you think it's unrealistic that one could be happy with the same person for fifty, sixty years?
Yeah. And I'll tell you why. You get *used* to each other. And as you get older, you're not looking for the same things anymore. I don't like to be bored with life. You've got to have a lot of passion and you've got to have a lot of *feeling.* Without feeling, there's nothing, it's just an act—and that's no good. You have to have that *urge.* And you *both* have to have it. You don't say, "We're going to have sex on Monday." *No.* He might come in from a golf match, all filthy dirty, and then all of a sudden you're in bed and you're having a hell of a time!

Be spontaneous.
Spontaneous, right!

What's the strangest thing a man has asked you to do?
Oh! Everything! And if you want to do it, you do it. If you don't want to do it, you say, "No, I'm not interested in that." That's

how simple it is. A man might say, "Suck me off." A lot of women like to do that. A lot of women *love* it. Some don't. A lot of men don't like to do that to the women, you know? It goes both ways.

I've asked everybody this question, but I have a feeling you're going to give me the straightest answer. Why does love die?
I'll tell you why. One of you drifts away. You have to have a lot in common to stay married. If he wants to go dancing and you don't want to go, well, that's okay occasionally, but don't do it every night because you can be sure that he'll find someone else to dance with.

How important is compromise?
Very. You have to give *all* of yourself to make the other person happy. But you have to make it so that you each *want* to give that much. Otherwise it's no good. A woman, if her husband's a golfer, she should learn to play golf. Otherwise, he's on the golf course all the time.

And if a woman likes to play bridge?
He should learn how to play, too. You're damn right. That's part of living together—teaching each other things.

More and more women are the ones asking for the divorces these days. Very different from your generation.
Right, the world today is completely different because the women are successful. A lot of women are more successful than their husbands. And that's not necessarily good for marriage. It's wonderful for women, of course, but if they become more successful than their husbands, it can be bad because then the man loses respect for himself. And then the husband becomes the pussycat—and that's no good. That's just my opinion. I could be wrong. I've been wrong plenty of times in my life.

Do you think the men are more like women these days?
I think so. I think men are much more interested in the way they look. *Much* more. I think they dress differently than they used to. They go to the gym. Now the women have to keep up with them!

Would you like to be a young woman in today's world?
Oh, yeah. Because I feel like I could keep up with any man. I'm not being conceited—don't misunderstand me. But I understand men. I do. My father, he always said to me, "If I was married to a woman like you, I'd own the world." He used to tell me that. I was the favorite, and I knew it. I could have had anything I wanted. I don't tell that to my brothers and sisters because I don't want to hurt their feelings.

"If you really want to open your eyes, you need to look at your own conduct and stop dwelling on what *they're* doing. That's the secret. That's like ten years of therapy right there in a nutshell."

ALIAS: John

OCCUPATION: Doctor

YEAR OF BIRTH: 1960

CURRENT MARRIAGE STATUS: Divorced

DO YOU HAVE ANY CHILDREN? Two teenage boys

WHERE YOU GREW UP: New York

WHERE YOU LIVE: New York

YEAR OF MARRIAGE: 1993

HOW LONG YOU DATED BEFORE YOU WERE MARRIED: Two years

YEAR OF DIVORCE: 2008

Looking back, were there a lot of red flags in your marriage, or did the end come as a shock to you?
It just flew in the face of: This is not the way my life is supposed to go. In my own delusional way I thought, "Why would she ever leave me? I have a big home and nice cars and we have a beautiful family and the kids are in a good school." It's like that whole "Why would anybody leave Elvis for the karate instructor?" That just doesn't happen, right? *Wrong.*

Many of the people I've interviewed for this book talk about change as a killer. Either they changed, or their spouse changed, or they were *hoping* their spouse was going to change and then they didn't. How do you really know who you're marrying?
The greatest piece of advice I would give is to spend a lot of time with your potential in-laws—somewhere where you can really see their interactions. Because in hindsight, I realize that my wife's mother beat the crap out of her husband. He was told

where to go and what to do, and he just sat there quietly. You wouldn't even know he was in the room. My ex's sisters are the same way—they just *browbeat* their husbands.

Did you feel like you were becoming that browbeaten husband?

As my marriage started to unravel, I began to do what all my divorced friends did in the final stages of their marriages. You become whatever it is you think your wife wants you to be. So yeah, that was the secret about my marriage. I became somebody I wasn't. And you're so inside the hole of it when things start to fall apart that you don't even see it coming. Toward the end I really didn't know *what* I was. In my mind, I was a fucking druid. I was an errand boy disguised as a husband.

How do you know when the marriage is over? When do you give up hope and stop trying to save it?

If I could give incredible advice it would be: Work on it, work on it, and work on it some more. Go home and talk about it. Do everything you can. And then when you get to that painful place where you know you can't do anything else—when you just know that it's deadly wrong—you make that hard right-hand turn and you get the fuck out. You focus only on yourself and you start moving in that healthy direction toward the sun.

What do you mean by "focus only on yourself"?

If you really want to open your eyes, you need to look at your own conduct and stop dwelling on what *they're* doing. That's the secret. That's like ten years of therapy right there in a nutshell. The second you start focusing on what they're doing, what they're not doing, how they're helping or not helping, who they're dating or whatever, you're driving yourself fucking nuts.

Were you compatible "on paper," or was it more of an opposites attract dynamic?

Opposites attract, it's a simple fact. And that's fine, there really is no need to agree on everyday things. My workout may not be her workout. I can find something to eat on the Thai menu even if I prefer a burger that night. What to watch on TV? Who cares? It's all irrelevant until you have children; then the "opposites attract" thing is a train wreck. And once we had children we couldn't see eye to eye and that became a daily fucking nightmare. And you're either going to fight that battle or you're just going to start watching from the hill. And that's when it turns into: *Happy wife, happy life.* Letting them do what they need to do. And if you're a guy, you start to smolder. You have an affair. Or you play lots of golf or you stumble off and you're just bitching and moaning all the time. Or you start drinking. I started running and taking ephedra.

Did you have an affair?

No. Never, ever. But I knew it was really bad when, after work, instead of going home, I'd go see a movie. Because I figured if I got home by nine, I could at least avoid the confrontation and come into a quasi-quiet home. I didn't even realize that was wrong. I didn't realize, Gee, I'm not going home after work, I'm going to see a movie—*alone*—and then lying about it. *Hello?*

Is it possible to avoid the elephants in the room, or will they always wind up crushing you in the end?

The avoidance thing, it just leads to an explosion. The cycle of withholding—I think that's a super-common dynamic. And then it becomes passive-aggressive and you start withholding things you would have given but now you're not because you feel that she's not. And then you start harboring resentments. And all of that comes back to the same thing: *communication.* But it's so hard to do.

Did you follow your own advice and do everything you could to save your marriage?

In hindsight, no, I could have done a lot more. But guys always miss it. You can be the brightest guy in town but when it comes to matters of the heart you can be a complete moron. There's just no correlation between intellect, business savvy, and love. Which is why there's a brain and there's a heart and there's about a foot and a half of space between the two.

Did any of your friends ever tell you that maybe she wasn't the right girl for you?

No. Because nobody talks about their real feelings toward their friends' spouses until they're actually, physically separated. You *can't*. You just can't say a word because if they work it out, you're Satan's cabana boy.

Would you go to your ex's funeral?

That's an incredible question. I would go to her funeral. But if something happens to my parents, I'm actually going to ask that she not attend. It's funny you ask that. You're the only person I've said that to. I don't hate her, it's just so awkward.

Is there a common fatal flaw that you've seen among your divorced friends?

At the end, it's always the same dynamic. Women are out of the marriage before the guy is. The guy finally figures it out, he tries to fix it, but it's so late in the game that it isn't fixable at that point. The girls I date now, they all tell me the same story. *He wasn't paying attention, he's trying now, but it's too late.*

What were some things that you tried doing to save your marriage?

I thought, "I'll take the whole family to Europe." If you have the funds to do it, you just start buying stuff, and not just jewelry—a new car, vacations. Guys in their simplest way think that that will actually fix it. It doesn't.

What could you have done that you didn't do?
I could have absolutely gotten into therapy sooner and communicated better and really gotten into some of the issues. But what did I do instead? Got up in the morning and ran. Got five miles in. Tried to get out of the house sooner so there wouldn't be any altercations. Tried to just smile a lot more. But I was smoldering.

Were you able to fall back on sex during the tough times?
You know, my ex was a terrible lover for me. She could be smoking hot for somebody else right now, and she probably is—she's getting boyfriend after boyfriend, so she's doing something right. But with me, it just wasn't happening. Maybe it was just all our pent-up energy and years of problems and confusion.

What about in the beginning?
Before we got married, we would have spontaneous sex everywhere. There wouldn't be any foreplay. She didn't do that. And once we got married, she still didn't do it. It was really just: *Get in there and get it done.* And foreplay is obviously a really great and important part of the sexual relationship. But there was no oral sex on her side of the fence. Dude, I'm gonna tell you that I never . . . I can't even say it because it makes me fucking cringe.

What?
I don't think I ever came in her mouth. *Ever.* That's over ten years of marriage. It just never happened.

Did you ever bring it up with her?
You want to know something? It really became a sore subject because then I'd get the speech. And it kills me now in hind-

sight because I must have been brain-dead. But she'd start talking about this car accident and how she had a TMJ problem. I actually heard this!

Is that a common complaint among your married friends? Not about oral sex necessarily, but that their sex lives are unsatisfying?
The most common thing I hear from my married friends is that their sex lives are destroyed. Are you married?

No.
No wonder—your skin, it looks so good. You're all clean, there's no lines and stuff. You have a girlfriend?

No.
You're in a magical place, man. Stumble around for a bit. Do your thing. Wear that fucking T-shirt. Drink a beer. Have some dim sum and enjoy your life.

Are you enjoying your life more now that you're single?
Oh, once you get separated you move on to other relationships and suddenly they're wonderful. I mean, I'm not going to show you pictures, but I could.

Pictures?
Oh, fuck it—*here*. Let me give you a taste of my world. I'm having the time of my life right now.

He pulls up a picture on his computer of a sexy girl, half-naked.

This is from this morning, she told me she wanted to play doctor. Seriously. This chick's thirty-five. She's kind of a Brigitte Bardot–looking girl with a gas station attendant mentality.

He pulls up another girl, gorgeous, from the neck down.

She didn't want me to take a picture of her face because she's separating right now from a divorce.

Another, this one younger.

This is the NYU Indian student.

Another.

This is this other chick who's chasing me and who is psycho.

Another.

This would be the hostess at the Four Seasons.

Can I see a picture of your ex-wife?
I'd show you but none exist.

Instead, he shows me a picture of another young woman—a brunette.

This is this unbelievable waitress from Gramercy Tavern who I actually really liked because she looked a lot like my wife did at twenty-three.

What does your ex think about you dating such young women?
Older women who have been divorced, when they see that you're dating a much younger girl, they want to rip your lungs out and stomp on your kidneys.

Do you think men have a bigger sex drive than women?
No, women have just as big a sex drive as men. The girl I was with last night was insane. Just out of her mind.

Of all these women you've dated, which one did you like best and why?

My favorite girlfriend was a nineteen-year-old from NYU. She had red hair and she was from Berkeley. She was too young but she was brighter than any girl I've bumped into. I could talk about Credence Clearwater, the Tet Offensive, Neil Armstrong, the Beatles' *Submarine* album. She was hysterical. And a fantastic lover. But I'm fifty-two, I have to go to sleep at about ten-thirty. I'm done. It's over. I was out last night until two in the morning with that chick in the first picture and I'm wiped. I'm destroyed. That's why I'm drinking coffee. But the point of all this is, and I'm not being mean here . . . now that I've had other lovers I realize that my ex was a *terrible* lover. If she had been one of the girls I'm currently seeing, I wouldn't see her anymore.

Looking at those pictures, it reminded me of that Matthew McConaughey line from *Dazed and Confused*. About how he keeps getting older but the girls just stay the same age. Do you feel that way?

Maybe what we were in high school, we are in life.

How do you mean?

I met this girl at the Soho House, she's a waitress there, twenty-five years old. She's a knockout. Smoking little blonde from Michigan. Last Sunday, I took her to the Bronx Zoo with her kid. She has a little kid. And I remembered back when I was twenty-eight I took a twenty-five-year-old girl up to the Bronx and did the exact same thing (except that one didn't have a kid). And I thought to myself, "What a magical life guys have." I can re-create myself. I can actually go back and date girls that are the same age as I was in 1987. It's insane. Women can't do that.

Maybe you should lead seminars on how to be single post-divorce.

Don't get me wrong, there are many nights that I go home alone. I'm not raging. I'm not Colin Farrell.

Are you lonely?
I'll tell you this, when you do go home alone, you walk in the front door, the kitchen doesn't smell of food, and the house is cold and dark because the heater hasn't been turned on. And I have a beautiful bedroom with a big white bed, and there's nobody in it. So I have this running joke: If I walk into my house and I'm alone, I yell, "Honey, I'm home!" And it just fucking echoes.

Do you want to get married again?
I don't want to get married again. And it's not because I want to run around, I just haven't quite figured out what exactly happened the first time. That's why I can never understand why my friends get married three or four times. That misses me like a fucking fly ball. How do you do this once and then you do it *again*? And then you get divorced and you do it *again*?

Okay, forget marriage—what about falling in love again?
I'm fifty-two years old, I'm three years away from being able to check into Leisure World. So yeah, you really do want to have someone in your life, and I don't want it to be a Filipino girl named Wind Song standing behind me in a wheelchair, you know? Plus, I have teenage sons. One's for sure going to get out of here as fast as he can and go to college. The other's going to move away. Suddenly I'm going to have five bedrooms and a fireplace and nobody's going to be there. And I don't want to be that creepy old guy sitting alone at the bar at the Kea Lani Hotel in Hawaii looking at the waitress.

"We all have fantasies in our head—it's when you *act* on them, that's the problem. If you don't want to cheat, you must avoid putting yourself in a situation where it can happen. *Duh.*"

ALIAS: Tasha

OCCUPATION: Retail

YEAR OF BIRTH: 1974

CURRENT MARRIAGE STATUS: Divorced

DO YOU HAVE ANY CHILDREN? No

WHERE YOU GREW UP: Illinois

WHERE YOU LIVE: Illinois

YEAR OF MARRIAGE: 2005

HOW LONG YOU DATED BEFORE YOU WERE MARRIED: Four years

YEAR OF DIVORCE: 2010

It's funny, my ex and I had a lot of the same habits, we loved the same TV and the same junk food. But in general we were complete opposites. I was the spoiled, better-educated, well-traveled, wild girl, and he was a meat-and-potatoes suburban boy—very basic. I always felt a little superior; I always had the upper hand. We got along, but I get along with everyone. In retrospect, we were not compatible at all. I mean, who doesn't like TV and junk food?

I guess I changed after the marriage, or maybe I just showed my true colors. When I met him I was not particularly attracted to him, he just grew on me—maybe because I knew that he worshipped me and that I could dominate him. I always dated people that were not challenging. Even before I married him, I told my friends and family that I would get my intellectual stimulation from them.

He wasn't stupid; he just wasn't interesting or worldly at all. It really annoyed me how his lower lip drooped when he was thinking about something—it made him look dumb, like Bubba from *Forrest Gump*. And he was always repotting the plants in the living room and hauling bags of soil around the apartment. It always seemed to happen the day after the housekeeper was there. Also, he looked really stupid in his mountain bike helmet, and he always used to close every single strap on his backpack and look like a total un-cool retard. I also noticed that he was kind of ugly and I didn't want to have his kids in case they would be ugly, too.

I know I sound like a total bitch. And it's funny because as I'm saying all this, and we've been apart for almost two years, it was all kind of endearing and maybe not so bad.

When you're dating you put more effort into yourself and the other person. Then, after you're comfortable for a while, things start to slip, you're not quite as nice. At least I'm not.

Yes, I hid my true nature from my ex. I acted like I'd had less sex than I did because I thought he would think I was slutty— which I kind of was at times. But he was pretty conservative, so I was hesitant to tell him some of the stuff I'd done. I'd let him think it was the first time with him. It's not that I was afraid of what he was gonna say, I just didn't want to . . . I don't know, I'm kind of fake with guys. I'm *still* fake with guys. Like, I hate the amount of people I've slept with so to this day I say I've only been with six or seven. And those dumbasses believe it. All girls lie about that—they're all a bunch of lying whores. But the point is, guys don't need to know.

I like keeping secrets, keeping a part of myself secret from men. We all have fantasies in our head—it's when you *act* on them, that's the problem. If you don't want to cheat, you must avoid putting yourself in a situation where it can happen. *Duh.*

I flirted with this guy at the gym for years, but when I knew he was gonna be at this party, I went, even though I should have known I couldn't trust myself. I could have avoided it, and probably should have. But I was weak, self-indulgent, disrespectful, and impulsive. We wound up having a major affair, and that was the beginning of the end of my marriage.

*   *   *

This new guy, he was a trainer at my gym. He was big and strong and had dreadlocks and he was always very clean and smelled good. We had this chemistry that I never had with my husband, just like, *I wanna jump your bones.* So there was this woman who was at the gym all the time, too, and she's like, "Oh, he has such a crush on you." Then one day, she had this party and she invited me.

So I went. I was hanging out, having some wine, and she's like, "Guess who's coming." And I was like, "Oh?" Like, I was excited. So he came up looking for me and we were like magnets. He stood next to me and just touched my leg, and it was like this electric current. And I was like, "Oh, shit!" Because I was going to Aruba the next day with my husband. This was after about six months of marriage.

So we fooled around that night in his car—we didn't have sex because I was still nervous, but we messed around *a lot.* And the next morning I went to Aruba. And I was totally not into my husband the whole time, because all I could think about was this guy. When we got back, it resumed. We were seeing each other every day.

Part of it was obviously that it was illicit. The other thing is that he was a different race. I'd never been with another race, so that was kind of a cool, wild experience. My husband was fine, we actually had decent sex, and it did get better with time. And I have to give him credit—here's something interesting that I find very manly about him. When you have your period, there are people who are like, "Okay, we're not having sex." Not only did he like having sex on my period, he'd *go down* on me. All the time. He *loved* it. And I was like, "If you want to, go ahead, I'm not going to stop you!"

But this new guy, physically, he had a much better body. Also, he was kind of hairless, which was weird. He didn't shave, he just wasn't hairy. And he did have a big penis. I mean, at first, I was *scared* of it. And the problem was that once we had sex, it was so much better, so then I wasn't into having sex with my husband anymore.

In the beginning, I was euphoric. I walked around singing, "I've got a husband *and* a hot boyfriend, who's better than me?" It felt awful in the moment when I had to lie or make up a story, but as soon as I was in the other place I could put it right out of my mind. I didn't get that feeling in my stomach until a few months into it when the boyfriend started nagging me to leave my husband, and then I just felt bad for both of them.

I was a fucking wreck, couldn't make up my mind. I woke up every morning with a stomachache. My hair was falling out—they say it happens after the stress. I was a total bitch to my husband. During the day, you busy yourself with work and friends, but when you're lying in bed with the person right next to you, you're just like, "What am I *doing*?" You have a constant torment, like, "I'm throwing away this great guy. Okay, so maybe I'm not gonna have wild and exciting men anymore, but at least I have someone that I can trust."

To this day my husband never found out. I actually went on five trips out of the country with this guy while I was married, and it's not like I traveled for work—*I freakin' worked at a store.* How the hell did I get away with it? I was a cheater and a liar, and it takes one to know one. That's why he never suspected me. Because he's not a cheater and a liar.

I'd like to believe in the fairy tale, but I think my head has been filled with too many romantic books and movies—and that doesn't exist. The problem is that I ate that shit up as a kid and teenager, and I expected all men to be like the guy from *The Princess Bride*. But they always disappointed me so I treated them like shit and cheated on them and didn't respect them.

After my wedding, one of my mom's friends came up to me

and said, "I noticed that you didn't say 'faithful' or 'forever' in your vows." And I was like, "Wow, you got that?" Thank God my husband didn't because it was totally intentional—I left both of those words out. To me, it was a wedding, not a marriage. I guess, somewhere deep down, I kind of knew. Boy, I really was just a selfish, immature asshole.

How have I changed since my divorce? I used to like wearing the pants. I liked to go out and work, I liked him to stay home and cook and clean. But that's not what I want anymore. In my mind and my body, I'm twenty-one—but in reality, I'm thirty-seven. I'm changing my tune. Now I want a man to be a man and I'm willing to be a woman. I've been going to an all-girls gym. I'm willing to wear a dress. I'll even cook!

Only recently have I realized that all this running around is kind of empty. Like, I was just really sick, and I couldn't open the NyQuil, and I was like, "You know, it would be nice to have someone to open the fucking NyQuil!" And I'm not getting any younger.

"You have to really be connected with someone to have sex on the hood of a car. You have to really feel safe."

ALIAS: Eddie

OCCUPATION: Media

YEAR OF BIRTH: 1972

CURRENT MARRIAGE STATUS: Divorced

DO YOU HAVE ANY CHILDREN? No

WHERE YOU GREW UP: New Jersey

WHERE YOU LIVE: Georgia

YEAR OF MARRIAGE: 2003

HOW LONG YOU DATED BEFORE YOU WERE MARRIED: Two and a
    half years

YEAR OF DIVORCE: 2008

You were thirty-one years old when you got married. Was that the right age for you?
No. Too young. I think a girl becomes a woman at twenty-nine, thirty, and a boy becomes a man at thirty-four, thirty-five. Most of the guys I know that got married before they were thirty are divorced, or they're cheating, or they're miserable. They're looking for a way out. But the ones who got married in their mid-thirties or later—most of them are happy.

How did you propose?
I took everything out of our living room and the dining room. We had wood floors, so from the minute you walked in, there were tea candles and white paper that wound all the way around to the living room. And there was a huge table there with flowers. I was dressed up in a nice suit and tie. No shoes. It was perfect. When she came home, she opened the door and said, "Oh, my God . . . I have to take a shit." That should have been a sign [laughs].

What happened when she came out of the bathroom?
I got down on my knee and proposed. I'd arranged it so that my parents and her parents were all flying in the next day for dinner. She was totally surprised.

When you were making the decision to propose, did you feel 100 percent certain that she was the right girl for you?
I'm a hopeless romantic. I really wanted it to work—I wanted to give her everything. I remember my uncle asked me, "Why did you buy such an expensive ring?" And I told him, "That's how much I love her." I actually borrowed money from my dad so I could get her a *bigger* ring. I ended up paying him $402.65 a month for four years straight.

Did you have any second thoughts on your wedding night?
My biggest fear was that we weren't going to consummate the marriage. Like, "Oh my God, what if we don't have sex?" Because that was a huge problem in our relationship. We did end up having sex, but she just laid there. I fucked her, I didn't make love to her.

What's the difference?
Making love requires foreplay. Being creative. Taking your time. Really getting wrapped up in the moment. It's passion. It's trust. That's so much better than fucking. Fucking is just sticking it in and getting it done. Even if you want to have quick sex in a dressing room, you can still *make love* in that dressing room.

Do you think sex is best when it's a little dirty? Like in a dressing room, for example?
When you respect each other, emotionally and spiritually, the things that you or I or the church or the rabbi might classify as "dirty"—I call that a deep connection. You have to really be connected with someone to have sex on the hood of a car. You have

to really feel safe. In my opinion, when you're really in love, then *nothing* is out of bounds. *Nothing* is dirty.

Were there things that you wanted to do with your wife but were too timid to ask?
No. Some men think they can't ask for what they want. They think maybe it's degrading. Like, if they want to fuck their wife in the ass. I think that's their own insecurity. You should be able to do anything you want with your wife or husband—assuming they're into it, of course. That should be your safe zone.

Was there anything you asked your wife to do that she wasn't into?
Anal sex. My wife would never even *consider* it.

Did that bother you?
A lot. Some of the most romantic moments of my life have been during anal sex.

Was the sex *ever* good between you two?
Not really, no. When we dated long distance for two years, I would fly to her city for the weekend and we wouldn't have sex the whole time. I remember standing at the edge of the bed and saying, "I'm up to here in cum! How come we're not having sex?"

Why would you marry her if you were so frustrated?
It's crazy, I know. But I loved her. I thought it would get better. Looking back on it, I probably loved the idea of marriage more than her.

Did the sex get better after you got married?
Worse. Again, it was never *good,* but when we first started dating, I would eat her pussy all the time. When we got married,

105

I stopped. No, *I* didn't stop—she stopped me. She didn't want it anymore. And I *loved* eating her pussy. I love eating pussy so much, you have no idea. But she was like, "Eh, come on." And I swear on my life as I look you in the eye: I never once came from a blow job. She would always just lick it for a minute and then sit on it. In seven years, I never had a full blow job.

Did you discuss that with her?
All the time. She would just say, "Okay." She was very manipulative. That's how I got my tattoo. We hadn't had sex for over a month and we were fighting and I said, "I'll do anything to stop fighting and have sex." And she goes, "Anything?" And I said, "Anything except convert to Catholicism or buy another dog." We had one dog at the time. And she said, "How about getting a tattoo?" And I said, "No." And she said, "Come on, get the tattoo." So I got the tattoo. And guess what? We *still* didn't have sex!

Were you watching a lot of porn during this relationship?
I'm not a porn guy. If you go to the cookies on my computer, I've never looked at a porn site in my life. It never turned me on. I don't need that.

Do you think men are kinkier than women?
No, I think women can be very kinky. But you have to put them in the right situation. You can't just expect your woman to be in Julia Roberts's high heels and a tie when you get home. You've got to make that happen. You've got to make her feel sexy and make her *want* to do that. But if you're not emotionally and spiritually connected, you're never going to get there.

Would you be okay with an open marriage?
No. I'm a traditional guy. But in the future, I need to make sure that I deal with the sex issues when they come up, as opposed to being spiteful.

How were you spiteful?

My ex didn't like to go out, she wasn't social, and I was in a business where I had to go out a lot: parties, weddings, concerts, dinners. There was family stuff, too: my mother's birthday, my sister's graduation. And she would never want to go. *Ever*. It was always a fight. I'd fly all over the world by myself. So every time I flew by myself, I was so angry with her, so upset and distraught, that I would go and fuck a hooker.

Just hookers?

No, I cheated with my partner's secretary. And I took my hairdresser to a hotel that was across the street from where I lived. Fucked her in the hotel, showered, then at three-thirty in the morning, went home and got into bed next to my ex-wife.

You felt like that was justified?

No. And I hope to never cheat again. But if you're not getting it at home, you're going to get it somewhere else.

Do you consider being with a hooker cheating?

Yes. And I don't ever want to be with another hooker.

How many have you been with?

I can't count. Over a hundred. My first prostitute experience was when I was twenty-two. I was at my buddy's bachelor party, he was the first one of us to get married, and I paid for a two-on-one. I was fucking some girl while the other one was licking my balls. I've never done coke, but hookers have always been my cocaine. But I have to tell you, as I've gotten older, I really don't have any interest in that anymore. I'm done with it.

Still, that's a lot of hookers. Why so many?

I wasn't happy at home. But instead of really dealing with it and getting help, I was just like, "She's not fucking me, so I'm going to fuck." Which is horrible, I realize. Why couldn't I have just said, "I'm not happy; we need to fix this or move on"? That would have been so easy. That's why it's so much better to just be really up front in the beginning. Like, "Look, this is who I am, okay? This is what I need."

Why didn't you do that?
Fear of rejection, I guess. It's hard to shake that security blanket. Instead, I carried it around for years. My black trainer always says, "You white people like to keep all this shit up your butt." Meaning, we sweep stuff under the rug, we don't like to confront our problems. And it's those situations, when you're not secure in your relationship, or you're not secure with yourself, that the demons inside just eat you alive.

How do you maintain the passion in a long-term relationship?
I think passion comes from compatibility and respect. It's not the other way around—it's a one-way street. And I never made the time or the effort. It takes work. You have to keep it romantic. And "romantic" doesn't have to mean candles and flowers and getting all dressed up. You can bring home a pizza and make that romantic.

And you never did things like that?
No. I would just avoid, avoid, avoid.

Your parents went through a nasty divorce. How did that affect you?
As much as I love my father, and I would do anything in the world for him, I think the way he talked about my mother definitely hurt me. Telling me that my mother was a piece of shit and a loser. He should have never disrespected her in front of me. My mother never talked that way about him. If I ever have

kids and get divorced, I will never talk badly about their mother in front of them, no matter what.

Your father was angry?
Oh, yeah. The one who gets left is angry. With me, it was the opposite. I left, but in my head I was always pushing her down as the bad one. It took me a long time to be able to look in the mirror and say, "You know what? You weren't so great, either."

"He just asks for exactly what he wants and I can do the same. There's no shame. Sexy outfits, naughty texts, it's just like, 'Hey, whatever turns you on, sure, let's try that!'"

ALIAS: Lulu

OCCUPATION: Film business

YEAR OF BIRTH: 1963

CURRENT MARRIAGE STATUS: Divorced

DO YOU HAVE ANY CHILDREN? A son, twelve years old

WHERE YOU GREW UP: California

WHERE YOU LIVE: Texas

YEAR OF MARRIAGE: 1996

HOW LONG YOU DATED BEFORE YOU WERE MARRIED: Four years

YEAR OF DIVORCE: Separated in 2007, divorced in 2010

I was twenty-nine years old. I'd spent a few years in Hollywood in the film business and needed a break. I was looking for a change in my life. I had a boyfriend from college named Alex who sort of tortured me for about ten years and he had moved to Vermont so I decided to go and see if there was anything for me to do there, workwise. I'd gone there every summer since I'd known him and had really fallen in love with the place. I ended up meeting with the owner of a film school and by the end of the interview he offered me a job and asked me to move from Los Angeles.

I decided to do it mainly to see if that relationship was going to work out or not. All of my friends thought I was nuts. I was moving to this tiny town in the middle of nowhere in the middle of winter for this guy who made me crazy. I rented a room in this incredible house right on a lake. It was all just so idyllic and picturesque, I felt like I was living in a movie about this big-city girl who goes off to a little town to find her true love. And just like a movie, there was a very unexpected twist.

On my first day of work, I walked into the building and there was this tall, handsome guy working there. His name was Oliver and he was a photographer. And that's the man I wound up marrying.

He grew up in Vermont and had always wanted to get out so I think there was an appeal in me that I had done and seen and been to all these places around the world. We were interested in a lot of the same things and we just bonded. It was a very sweet . . . I guess you'd call it a courtship. We saw each other every day. He wrote me these incredible letters and notes and cards and he was thoughtful in ways that were very specific to me. At the time, I thought he was the perfect antidote to the pain and struggle I'd been going through with Alex. *What's the better choice here? What am I getting more out of?* It was a no-brainer.

With Alex, I was so truly in love with him, but there was no consistency. He was emotionally hot and cold—"I love you, I love you, but I can't commit to you." A lot of pushing and pulling and being together and then not. The sex was very central to our connection, while some of the other parts weren't as developed. But with Oliver, it was the reverse. There was definitely an attraction there, but it wasn't as intense. It was very comfortable. Very loving, very safe. At the time I thought, "This is more balanced, it's not supposed to be this crazed, lustful thing all the time—you're supposed to be more calm."

Talking about it now, with perspective, I'd have to say that when you're married you absolutely *need* that lustful thing to fall back on. Because there's so much mundane stuff living with somebody day in and day out, you have to be able to get back to that original place of *I can't keep my hands off this person.* And from the very beginning, Oliver and I just didn't have that. I guess I just kind of rationalized and accepted it.

The sex you have in your twenties is so different from the sex you have in your forties. It's like a whole other experience. It wasn't *bad* in my twenties but it's so much better now. Because you know what you want and what works for you. I think a lot of women aren't asking for what they want because they're still concerned about how they'll be perceived. The person I'm with now, he's so uninhibited, it really makes it easy for me to be the same way because there's no fear and no embarrassment. He just asks for exactly what he wants and I can do the same. There's no shame. Sexy outfits, naughty texts, it's just like, "Hey, whatever turns you on, sure, let's try that!"

Marriage sex is a whole other thing. It's really hard to maintain those early levels of passion and intensity. When it's just the two of you, if you have a good sex life, that will continue for as long as you want to make it a priority. The challenge comes when you have a child.

That first year after you have a kid is all about survival. And I don't know a lot of couples who are having much sex. The underlying thing you have to know is that, as the husband, you are totally displaced. And that's a bummer. I have male friends who I love and adore who've been married for years who went and had an affair during that year because they just felt like: "Where *am* I now?" The baby gets so much love and attention and the mother gets so much satisfaction from the child—there's just not a lot left for somebody else. And you're exhausted and tired and you don't feel sexy. So if you can get through that year and get back to your old self, then I think you'll be okay.

The other thing I learned is that the idea that you have control over someone else is a fantasy. The truth is that every day you have to make a conscious decision to be in the relationship fully. You have to remain an active participant and pretend a little like you haven't signed this legally binding document. Like you're there because you *choose* to be, not because you *have* to be.

Consistency is really important—you don't want to feel hung out to dry—but isn't it the ultimate spiritual enlightenment to live in the moment, not the past or the future? I think most people strive for comfort and transparency and to relax totally in their relationships. Like, *Phew, that's over—I found this person and I don't have to think about it anymore, I'm done!* For me, I like having a little bit of that *not* knowing. I like a little chase, a little mystery, a little uncertainty. It's good to keep each other on your toes.

Someone once said to me, "When a woman decides to get out of a marriage, it's over. A man, instead of getting out, will have an affair." And that was true for me. I guess you can choose to believe that there's one person for you and that's your destiny or you can believe that there might be a series of people who are right for you at different points of your life.

I now have more freedom than ever before. I get to make a choice in every relationship: *Does this person make me happy? Is this working for me?* When you hear people talk about "dropping off the cliff" after a divorce or saying "it's all downhill from here"— I don't feel like that at all. New worlds have opened up to me in so many other ways.

"If somebody really wants to do something, they're going to do it. You can say, 'I don't like that, I wish you wouldn't, that would make me feel bad.' But you can't fight against it. You're just not going to win."

ALIAS : Ben

OCCUPATION: Financier

YEAR OF BIRTH: 1973

CURRENT MARRIAGE STATUS: Divorced

DO YOU HAVE ANY CHILDREN? No

WHERE YOU GREW UP: Indiana

WHERE YOU LIVE: North Carolina

YEAR OF MARRIAGE: 2002

HOW LONG YOU DATED BEFORE YOU WERE MARRIED: Year and a
half

YEAR OF DIVORCE: 2009

Tell me something that you absolutely have to love about the person you're going to marry.
I think it's really important that you love to hear the sound of their voice. I always liked how Celine's voice sounded. Even if I sometimes hated what was coming out of her mouth, there was always something about her voice that I totally loved. I *still* love the way her voice sounds.

When did you first hear it?
In the late '90s. I'd been living in Italy and I'd gotten together with this girl named Daphne. We had a little relationship; it was nothing serious. Then I left, a couple years went by, and I was visiting again. So we made plans to meet up at this huge warehouse rave, and she had a friend, Celine, who was meeting us there.

Were you attracted to Celine when you met her?
I thought she was gorgeous. Not model beautiful—she was

uniquely beautiful. But no, I felt nothing at the time, and neither did she. We barely even spoke that night. I was so completely focused on the other girl.

Two years after that I was back in Italy for business. Things were totally over with Daphne. I was standing at the top of this staircase and a girl came up to me and said, "I remember you." It was Celine. We wound up going to a bar and meeting up with my friend George, and then later we all went to a club. But when we got there, they were just totally into each other, huddled in a corner, talking the whole night. So at two o'clock in the morning I was like, "Okay, see ya, guys—I'm leaving."

I went back to my friend's house where I was staying. We were sitting in the kitchen drinking wine at four o'clock in the morning and then all of a sudden I heard my name being yelled from outside. So I was like, "What?" I walked outside and Celine was standing there in the middle of the street. And I was like, "What's going on? Where's George?"

And she said, "I threw him out of the car."

I said, "I don't understand. What are you doing here?"

And she said, "I like you. I thought there was something between us."

Did you feel that, too?
No. I had no idea there was anything between us. I assumed she was getting together with George! But I thought, "Wow, this is really courageous." I started seeing her in this whole new way, which was fascinating. She just seemed so genuine. And I remember thinking, "I've never met anyone like this before. I'm really curious who this person is."

When you meet someone and you start falling in love with them, what is it that you're ultimately hoping will happen?
What you really hope for is to find someone who, despite all your bullshit, is able to recognize something about you that they

feel connected to. And from the very beginning, Celine gave me the most amount of genuine love that I'd ever felt from another person. The intensity, the depth—she was just so committed—it was inspiring to see how much passion she had.

Was there a downside to that passion?
Yes. We fought like crazy. There were more broken dishes and destroyed cabinets and people storming out of cars than in any other relationship I've ever been in. She was able to bring out anger in me that I didn't know existed, which was not entirely a bad thing. I actually really respected her for it because I'm usually not like that at all. I would be the reticent one—reserved, cautious, guarded—whereas she just expressed herself without any fear of the consequences.

Can you give me an example?
After we were married, we were living in Manhattan, and she decided that she didn't like my mom anymore. And I was like, "Well, you don't really have that option, we're a married couple, we go to Thanksgiving together." But she was like, "No, I don't want to, I don't have to like her, I don't have to go." Now, it's totally normal that wives don't get along with their mother-in-laws, but I was like, "Can you just go and pretend to be happy, or at least just not make it awkward? Can you please just do that—for me?" But she couldn't. One time she tried and it was almost worse. We had to leave early and the look on my mom's face was just so disappointed.

Your parents got divorced when you were a kid. What did you learn *not* to do by watching them?
The big thing I learned from my parents' divorce is that there are certain things you just can't fight against. If somebody really wants to do something, they're going to do it. You can

say, "I don't like that, I wish you wouldn't, that would make me feel bad." But you can't fight against it. You're just not going to win.

How do you fight productively?
You have to be honest. I think we tend to avoid and withhold a lot of stuff in our daily lives just to keep things going smoothly. We pick our battles; we don't want to rock the boat. So you have to create a forum where it's okay to say all the things you can't say normally. Fighting is like the court or the ring or the arena. There are boundaries but it's still full-contact. And once you enter that arena, that's the time to let it all out.

But letting it all out requires a lot of vulnerability—admitting what bothers you. Are you ever afraid of being seen as needy?
Yeah. And maybe I have a weird view of women nowadays, but I don't think they want you to be needy. They want to *desire* you, they don't want you to be demanding of their attention. I think they rebel against that kind of clinginess. They don't want to be required to do something, they want to *feel* it.

Same with sex?
Yeah. You really have to *want* the other person.

How do you maintain that desire over the years?
Well, in a long-term relationship it goes through different phases. At the beginning there's lots of kissing, just touching each other, and that's exciting for a while. But as time goes on, and you've done everything over and over again, it can start to feel dull or like maybe there's something better out there. I was guilty of feeling that, for sure. I became a little complacent and I think women pick up on that immediately.

Would you say that you had a good sex life overall?

Overall, I think we had a pretty good sex life. It didn't ever feel tame or redundant or like we were just going through the motions. There was desire. It was passionate. It was physical. It wasn't all centered around the groin, like, "Okay, we're fucking." She was actually pretty uninhibited, which I liked.

How so?

She was into the idea of being dominated. Being degraded. She had fantasies of being a prostitute. In a safe way, not violent. That turned her on. To be really proper and beautiful on the outside but on the inside . . .

Were you okay playing out that role?

Yeah. Sometimes you need something soft and sweet and sometimes you need to be a little bit destructive, you know?

Did you ever want to switch roles?

No. I definitely don't want to be degraded. I don't think so, anyway; nobody's ever really asked me.

Many of the people that I've interviewed said that they hid their true desires from their spouses. That they were afraid of rejection or being seen as freaky. How important is it to "discuss the dirty"?

Oh, you need to discuss those boundaries even if it upsets the other person. And to be honest, I don't know if we ever really did that, like really laid it all out on the table. Looking back, I wonder how much I actually knew about what she liked and didn't like. I know that she didn't want to do *every*thing.

Like what?

I don't think she'd want to have public sex. Or I don't think she liked the idea of dildos and toys.

Was there anything that you wished she wanted to do?
Um, yes. She didn't swallow my cum. I would have liked that. She would always just finish with a hand job.

Is that better or worse than spitting it out?
I think spitting it out is worse. It's almost mean. It's like, "Your cum is gross!" I don't think it's gross. Maybe it's a little dirty, but it's dirty in a good way. On the other hand, it's like, "Why do I need to have my cum swallowed?"

Were you always faithful to her?
Always. I never cheated on Celine. Even if I could have gotten away with it I wouldn't have because I'd feel like it would be damaging in some way; it would have consequences. It would upset the orbit of the relationship. It's not so much about hurting her—although it would—it's about protecting what you have together. The esoteric part is hoping that the other person is thinking the same thing, that there's some telepathy in love that happens where they wouldn't want to be doing that, either.

Did she ever cheat on you?
I don't know if she ever actually *cheated* on me. At the end, we were living in the same house but it was more like cohabiting. We were just angry at each other so I slept on the couch for about six months. And at a certain point, she said, "I don't know if I love you anymore." I felt like I had done everything I could to keep this relationship together, so I said, "Okay, then I have to go." So I moved out. And very soon after that I had a feeling that she was with somebody. So I drove by the house one night. The gate had a little walkway and you could see right into the kitchen window. And I saw some guy in a blue sweater doing the dishes.

How long did you watch for?
I stayed there for like fifteen seconds and then drove away. I

went to a bar. I just couldn't watch anymore. I didn't want to see too clearly who this person was.

Did you ask her about it?
A few weeks later, I went back to the house. I was helping her with something, and I went into the bathroom and there was a pregnancy test wrapper in the trash can. And I was like, "What is this?" Or probably more like, "What the fuck is this?" And she said, "It's Miriam's." Her friend. So I was like, "Oh, Miriam came over here and did a pregnancy test in your bathroom?" Eventually it came out that, no, it was hers. She'd been seeing this guy for, I don't even know how long. And then it got graphic. I asked her all these questions:

"So you're having sex?"

"What was it like?"

"Is he coming inside you?"

"Do you love him?"

"Are you saying 'I love you' to him?"

I made myself crazy for about two years. That kind of jealousy can become all-consuming.

There's an Alexandre Dumas quote, "The chain of wedlock is so heavy that it takes two to carry it—sometimes three." What goes through the mind of the person who gets left out?
The thing about cheating is, for the person who did it, it might have just been this meaningless sexual encounter. But in the mind of the person who was cheated on, it becomes this almost mythical thing. You're left with these images and you replay them over and over again in your imagination. I actually don't think a one-night stand is the worst thing in the world. I think having a relationship or an affair—keeping that kind of secret—is really bad. Because if there's that level of deception going on it really makes you start to question everything you thought was true about the other person. It's like, "Who are they? Do I really

know them? If they did this, what else are they capable of doing?" And it's really hard to recover from that kind of thinking.

Is Celine still together with that guy in the blue sweater?
Yeah.

Do you still speak to her?
Yeah, we still speak a fair amount. There was awhile when I really didn't want her calling me because it always made me feel like I was being used. Every conversation was "Hey, how are you? Can I ask you a favor?" But last week she called me, crying. She was really upset about something and for the first time I felt like she was calling me because she didn't have anyone else who she could depend on. And I thought, "Wow, that was really nice."

Did you wind up feeling better about everything?
Yeah, we laughed a little bit and it turned into a good conversation. We talked about our relationship in a way that wasn't painful. And after the conversation, I thought, "It would be great to have a genuine friendship with her." She can still make me incredibly frustrated, but I don't hate her. I don't regret marrying her at all and I totally want to get married again.

What if she came on to you?
I wouldn't do it. I know for a fact. It's just over.

How do you know?
I just don't have that feeling for her anymore. I can't believe it, but it's gone. I was so happy when I realized it was gone. It got transferred to somebody else. And it was such a fucking relief.

"I realized that I needed to be with someone who could at least *talk* about all the different parts of me and come clean about her own stuff as well."

ALIAS: Paul

OCCUPATION: Psychologist

YEAR OF BIRTH: 1961

CURRENT MARRIAGE STATUS: Remarried in the mid-'90s

DO YOU HAVE ANY CHILDREN? Yes, two, with my current wife

WHERE YOU GREW UP: Ohio

WHERE YOU LIVE: Florida

YEAR OF MARRIAGE: 1990, 1997

HOW LONG YOU DATED BEFORE YOU WERE MARRIED: Two years,
     two years

HOW LONG YOU WERE MARRIED: Almost three years, fifteen years and
     counting

YEAR OF DIVORCE: 1993

How would you describe yourself in terms of your sexual identity?

I'm a cross-dresser. People like me, along with transsexuals, make up the transgender community. I'm not traditionally bisexual; my bisexuality comes from being trans. In terms of how that affects my identity, it's as much a part of who I am as my ethnicity, maybe more.

To be clear: Anatomically speaking, you're all man.

Yes.

And you're married to a woman. But you like to dress in female form, and when you do, you're attracted to men.

Yes.

And *only* when you're dressed as a woman? Traditional gay sex doesn't appeal to you at all?
Not at all.

Sitting here now you look like a pretty regular guy. Have you had any surgeries to enhance your feminine side?
Lots of little adjustments. I've had my nose done, redone, and then redone again over the years. I've had my brow lifted and then relifted. The corners of my chin, where they jutted forward, I had them shaved down. To truly look more convincing as a woman I'd have to take the squareness out of my jaw and make my chin smaller in general. And that would be a tough thing to do. You don't mess with handsome male features unless you want to be a woman full-time.

And you like being both?
I like both. I've worked hard to set up the life I lead.

You obviously have a tremendous amount of trust and freedom in your current marriage. Do you think it's true that the unleashed dog stays closer to home?
The unleashed dog who is *happy at home* stays close to home. Allowing your spouse more freedom can contribute to their happiness but I don't think it's the key.

In my interviews for this book, the words "work" and "compromise" come up constantly. It seems that newlyweds often go through a period of fairy-tale withdrawal, of adjusting their expectations. What's a bit of advice you'd give to young couples that are dealing with that type of adjustment?
You have to re-earn it every year. *Oh, I'm married and secure and blah blah blah.* No—you earn your keep *every* year. Neither goes complacent. That doesn't make for a quality relationship. That's

people getting dismissive or being insensitive toward each other. That's people getting fat or nasty on each other. That's not caring.

How did you meet your first wife? Tell me the love story.
The love story, yes. Well, I came out of college at twenty-two, overworked and unhappy, and moved to Florida for graduate school. And I found that the forces in the dating market had shifted. Romantically, women rule the world until about the age of twenty-three, twenty-four. Because it's a world driven by sex appeal. But as you get older, it becomes a world driven by *catch appeal*. And all of a sudden I was pretty sought after as opposed to being, like, "Hey, how come I'm always one of the better-looking men but all the prettier women are getting snatched away by the older, the smoother, the wealthier, the more athletic?" So I was determined to finally find the type of woman who I would see and just want to sweep off her feet and throw her down for a romp in the hay. The type of woman who just incited lust in me. And then I fell head over heels for a French-American woman named Barbara. A friend introduced us. She worked in fashion.

You immediately wanted to sweep her off her feet?
Absolutely. She represented that type of exotic beauty for me.

And how about the romp in the hay?
Unquestionably. I'd want to throw her down right then, there, wherever. She was *gorgeous*. And she was extroverted whereas I was introverted, and that's exciting.

Was that lust mutual? Did she want to throw you down as well?
I think she loved me as a catch, like, "Whoa, I've got a big fish on the line here." So we both had our reasons and just fell for each

other like two large, gravitational objects. We were just thoroughly taken with our ideas of each other.

How was the sex?
I couldn't get enough. She was Mona Lisa to me. Just touching her, she was like the softest velvet. Just holding her, she had this kind of pliability that molded into my shape and fit me like a glove. And she was definitely a girl's girl, a hyperfeminine kind of woman, and that's hot to me. It's hot to most guys, I think.

Hyperfeminine. How so?
Just all the little things she would do with her hands and her body, the way she would talk. And she would really pay attention to her hair and makeup and what she wore each day. But not in a cheap way, in a very classy way, like she hadn't paid much attention to it at all—and that's sort of the perfect crime [laughs]. She also did all these silly, giddy, childlike, make-a-big-deal-out-of-the-holidays types of things. I wanted to pick her up and hug her and kiss her when she was dyeing Easter eggs as if she was on methamphetamines—it was just *so exciting*. That stuff kills me.

You said you were taken by your *ideas* of each other. Can you recall an example of when your real selves started to show through?
We went on our first trip together to see a friend of hers who was getting married. So we were driving and I said something like, "This is great. I just love what we've got going together—I haven't been this happy since my days with Susan back in high school." And it was as if I'd just struck her across the face. She lost it. "Don't you know you cannot talk about an ex-girlfriend around a woman that you're seeing! That is cruel! Shut up now!"

Had you ever seen her so angry?
No. There was a brittleness to her that I had never seen before.
I was stunned.

At this point in your life, you still had never been with a man or dressed up as a woman?
No, other than the rare, borrowed bra or panty or old sweatshirt that I'd stretch down to my knees until it felt like the dress Jennifer Beals wore in *Flashdance*. In private moments, essentially.

Masturbating?
Right.

What would you fantasize about?
The fantasies that were the hottest for me were like, some guy is innocently going about his business and he's trapped and forced or manipulated into just the kind of thing that turns me on. You know, forced feminization. Those things really get me on a gut-punch level. Being the victim. *It wasn't his idea, he was kidnapped and they had all these nefarious things in store for him!*

Why *forced*? Because without consent there's no complicity? There's no blame or guilt if you didn't choose to do it?
Exactly, I now realize. It really takes the responsibility off your shoulders.

Growing up, did you embrace that kinkier side of yourself, or did you try to bury it?
Well, the human mind is a nimble thing and we can tell ourselves stories to make the problematic stuff go away. I told myself a lot of stories. I mean, I knew I was the guy who had this weird sexual turn-on, but I thought, "Hey, guys have weird fantasies. Who the hell knows what they think about when they masturbate?"

Were you an effeminate kid?

No, growing up I was boyish. I was good at sports. I felt like a fairly regular straight dude and was kind of stunned when I went through puberty and discovered that some of my sexual interests involved raiding my sister's panty drawer. Also, I had a female roommate for one of my years in grad school and sometimes it was, like, "Hmm, I wonder what it'd feel like to wear something like that."

Was it just a superficial curiosity or did you think it was something deeper?

It was all about curiosity, sexual fantasy, and envy. Curiosity first, sexual fantasy as I went through puberty, and then these weird envies. Like wanting to wear a skirt and be hot—and I mean like *people can't keep their eyes off you* hot. Like the pretty woman that Roy Orbison sings about. The type that stops traffic. I would think of it as *Venus* envy. Vagina envy. I remember learning the term "penis envy" and I was like, "Um, I kind of have the opposite of that."

You wanted to be that object of desire?

Yes, that's a big element of true female sexuality, the desirability thing. The ultimate thing for me was some sort of "Him Tarzan, me Jane" experience. Like somebody just *has* to look at me and touch me and then he's exploding inside me, which is the ultimate mark of "I just made magic happen for someone."

And what about your sexual attraction to women? What turns you on?

I kind of like everything about women—how they look, how they move, how they express themselves. A lot of my sex drive for women is a sort of vicariousness. Like, I'm going to do everything to this woman that I would like done to me—and with *style*.

You mentioned that you had a female roommate in grad school. Would you secretly wear her clothes when she was out?
Well, it all started with my sister's stuff. And don't get me wrong, I felt plenty bad about it. It's just so *wrong*. As an adult looking back, I'm like, "God, I would never mess with anybody's stuff—it's so creepy!" But these were desperate times. Seriously exciting, seriously disturbing. And there was all this guilt and shame, like, "What's wrong with me? Does this mean that I'm gay?" I clung to my story of being this twisted straight guy, but could it mean I'm far freakier than that? Could it somehow mean that I'm transsexual?

Did you ever try to share any of this with Barbara? Or to bring elements of your fantasies into the bedroom?
I did. One time, we were about to have sex and she went off to the bathroom to freshen up. While she was gone I put on her underwear, and when she came back, I was like, "Hey, look at me, I'm a muscle woman! Ha-ha-ha!" And she was *aghast*. She was like, "Take that stuff *off*—that is *not funny*. I never want to see you do anything like that ever again!"

How did that make you feel?
I was certainly rather embarrassed. I was taking a risk and the dice came out snake eyes. Or at least not the double sixes I was hoping for. I realized then that there wasn't going to be any of this part of me in my marriage so I sort of stashed it away.

How did it eventually come out?
I was interviewing for internships so I was starting to take a lot of out-of-town trips.

Uh-oh.
Right. Out-of-town trips—*look out*! So on one trip, to Denver, I met a woman and she was real nice, pretty, and staying at the

same hotel. We decided to have dinner together, and in looking at her I was thinking that it would be nice to have a last hoorah, to utilize my freedom one last time before I surrender it forever. And I fully intended to surrender it forever. So while she went off to the ladies' room, I thought to myself, "Is there anything you'd like to do while you still have the chance?" I'd been with a decent number of women, so I thought, "It's not worth breaking my vows or my loyalty to Barbara for something I've already done." But that question was to bang around in my head incessantly.

"Is there anything you'd like to do while you still have the chance?"
Right. It was bulletined throughout my entire mind and body. *Now, or forever hold your peace.* And it really awoke the demon child inside of me. It was like, "I hate it, but a part of me wants—no, forget *wants*. A part of me *needs* to know what it's like to be a woman with a man just once—*just once*—before I lose that option forever." It became like this two-ton boulder weighing down on my soul. I knew I'd never sleep soundly until I could make that urge go away.

How did it go from an urge to a plan to reality?
I knew a gay guy who had lived down the hall from me at my previous apartment building. He was kind of a silly guy, but one evening after dinner I went over to his place to get some coffee. He knew I was getting married, and while I was there I confessed to him that I was curious to experiment with a man before it was too late. And he's like, "You're kind of hot, you can experiment with me right here if you'd like!"

Were you attracted to him?
Not at all. He was weak-chinned and scrawny but there were larger stakes in play here. So he turned off the lights, stood next to me, and started to kiss me. I had to force myself to kiss and hug him back. It was terribly awkward. A man's body feels dif-

ferent, it's sort of a stack of two-by-fours as opposed to a mold of Jell-O, like my fiancée. But I was very eager to give oral sex. That seemed like one of the most womanly things one could do.

More to give than to receive?
Oh, hell yeah. There's nothing female about having somebody suck your cock. But receiving intercourse, that has always seemed like the ultimate female sexual act.

So . . . did you?
Yeah, that all happened that night.

Was it all that you dreamed it would be?
It certainly wasn't. I was under a lot of pressure and didn't have the luxury of being as safe as I would have liked to be.

Did he use a condom?
Well . . . this guy just couldn't fuck with a condom. He tried but he couldn't stay hard enough. He was like, "I've got a good sense of timing and I can pull out." And that pushed me into a huge dilemma: "I'll either have to do this horribly awkward experiment again or else just find a way to push through it so I can move on with my life. Because this is just a temporary, little, quirky interest that I'm getting out of my system before I get married, right?"

That's what you genuinely thought?
Yeah, a weird last hoorah. Not a hoorah I would want to talk about with anybody, but one that I desperately needed. So I went with it.

How did it feel?
It felt really different to be on the other end of the stick, so to speak. It hurt a little bit. The tightness. It was uncomfortable. So

I thought, "I didn't even like it and I exposed myself to this scary risk. At least I got it out of my system." But a part of me *knew*. The moment I was entered the way a man would enter a woman, it opened up something very real inside of me.

Were you happy that you did it?
Yes, at first. But I went on to feel like I had done the most horrid, dangerous, cruel, irresponsible thing ever when . . . well, my fiancée started to have all this genital itching and discharge. And it upset me like nothing else ever had before—or since—in my life. I started to get panic attacks with a lot of physical symptoms, which I knew overlapped a little bit with acute retroviral syndrome.

What's that?
It's something people get within two to six weeks of becoming HIV-positive. It's like a bad flu. And being somewhat medically savvy, I knew just enough to be worried and it totally flipped me out. My mind never had more than ten minutes' rest before I was back on this topic: *Oh my God, I could have killed myself and killed Barbara in the process.*

Did you eventually end up telling her everything?
Yes.

***Everything* everything?**
Eventually. She saw me suffering and was like, "Gosh, what is it? You can tell me, it's okay." Then I made the full confession.

Did she freak?
She lost her fucking mind. Her shoes were off, and she grabbed one of them and whipped it hard against the wall, denting the thing. She ripped her engagement ring off, threw it on the

ground, and stormed off. She was like, "What a crock of shit! What sort of pathetic sham of a man are you? Get away from me, I don't know who you are!" Which was certainly a reasonable thing to say at the time.

Wait, back to the itching and the discharge. Had you contracted an STD and given it to her?
You know what? It turned out that her doctor had changed the antibiotics she'd been taking for frequent UTIs. And changing a woman's antibiotics can cause a yeast infection.

So it was just a huge spook?
It was Desdemona's handkerchief. Yeah, it was a whole lot of nothing that led me to change the course of history.

Wow. Okay, so you enter therapy, you get married, you're living together.
Yes.

And did that experiment with the guy turn into a thorn in your relationship or was it more like, "Let us never speak of it again"?
We had a few clashes because of the way she lashed back at me for it. She just felt that this experiment was something I had done *to her*. And she would just lose it. "You cheated on me!" I would try to explain, "There was a part of me that existed before you that was always curious. I had to deal with it as honorably as I could, which meant getting it out of the way before it would be adultery, before it would be ripping a whole family apart." And she was like, "Oh! How can you even *talk* about it?" And *boom*— she'd storm off. Because ultimately she just wanted to banish the whole experience—never mention it again. *The noose in the house of the hung.*

Were you starting to question your long-term compatibility?
Yes, the tide was turning. I felt like I had no freedom of speech with her. And I worried whether she was sophisticated enough for a special-needs case like me.

But you dated for years. Why did it take you so long to figure this out?
I had hoped to find it in her, but I didn't. Cross-dresser or not, I guess there was a part of me that always wanted to be a hippie or an independent filmmaker and just say, "Screw the culture, man, let's just talk openly about what's really going on!" So for reasons like that, I loved therapy. And Barbara was like, "This sucks, I'm fine—F-I-N-E." And you know what that stands for, right? *Fucked up, insecure, neurotic,* and *emotional.* Oh, yeah, if you're those four things and you're not ready to admit it, you're *fine.*

Barbara couldn't talk openly about what was really going on?
No, not at all. In my therapy, I had developed a taste for a deeper level of sharing in relationships. And I realized that I needed to be with someone who could at least *talk* about all the different parts of me and come clean about her own stuff as well. And I just couldn't let that go.

You were married to Barbara for almost three years. During that time, did you ever have any other experiences dressing up as a woman or any other sexual interactions with men?
No. Maybe if she was out of town I might borrow something, like a negligee, just to get off. That was it. Because none of those things were really possible in my marriage. Even something I might allow myself to do in private, that was a bad idea because it was against the law according to the woman I lived with. And *law-schmaw* in some sense, but these things were *unethical.*

Unethical according to whom?

According to the laws of our marriage. If you have understand-ings and agreements with somebody, to then go out and violate them—that's wrong. I don't care about Judeo-Christian mar-riage, I don't care about some of the laws in this country. But when you promise somebody that you're not going to behave in a certain way, then you don't just go off and do whatever you want. And these things that I wanted to do, they were illegal—they were *unethical*—when I was living with Barbara.

Is that why you ultimately left? So you could be free to be yourself?

Yes. I wanted a marriage where I could say, "You know what? Damn it, there are times when I just wish I was Cindy Crawford and I can't help it! Don't *you?*" I wanted to be able to *say* things like that so that I wouldn't have to feel so bad about who I was. So I could just feel like, "Okay, it's weird, but what the hey? People are weird."

Have you come to terms with your weirdness?

I know that I'm seen by many as this freaky, sexual kind of guy. But the truth is, I'm a relatively conventional person who got drafted into this by birth. I didn't want to be such a "kinky bas-tard," I really didn't.

Your current wife, you told her everything before getting married?

Yes.

***Everything* everything?**

Yes, *everything*.

How? What did you tell her, exactly?

That I have to be able to be a woman sexually with a man sometimes. I said, "You would always come first, I would always be super careful, and I don't need to tell any of our friends about this. But I really need to do this." *No abandonment. No endangerment. No embarrassment.* Those are the three big rules. I said, "I love you and I want a life with you but I don't think I can keep going forward if you can't find a way to make this legal."

Did she freak?
She sure swallowed hard. But she didn't jump up from the table, she didn't lose control and have some sort of tantrum. She said, "I'll have to think about this."

That was fifteen years ago?
That was fifteen years ago.

You're a lucky man. And a lucky woman, too.
Thank you [laughs]. You know, I'm so fortunate that any of these kooky, crazy, unlikely, surreal things have been possible. It has made certain periods of my life feel like heaven on earth.

"Whenever you're living in passion, you're living in the fear that you're going to lose something. And if you live in that fear all the time, you're not acting out of your heart."

ALIAS: Marion

OCCUPATION: Teacher

YEAR OF BIRTH: 1971

CURRENT MARRIAGE STATUS: Divorced

DO YOU HAVE ANY CHILDREN? Yes, a son, fourteen

WHERE YOU GREW UP: Kentucky

WHERE YOU LIVE: Vermont

YEAR OF MARRIAGE: 2002

HOW LONG YOU DATED BEFORE YOU WERE MARRIED: Two years

YEAR OF DIVORCE: 2006

I met my husband the day I got out of a seven-year relationship with the father of my son. He and I had spent New Year's Eve together and then I was like, "It's over." So I went out for a drink with my girlfriend and this guy passed by and saw me in the window and he knocked. He came in and put his business card down and said, "I want to see you. I want to spend time with you." Very cocky. I was attracted to the fact that he was very sure of himself, that he had the balls to come up and approach me in that way. The entire marriage was like that.

He was on TV and he was fifteen years older than I was. Big ego, very domineering. And I was lost and looking for a father figure, so we fit perfectly. We started out having a lot of fun. I fell in *lust*—there was a real physical chemistry. Even now when I see him there's that attraction. But when I really watch him I don't know what I was doing with a guy like that. He was just really damaged. He had a bad temper and serious drug and alcohol problems. Coke, ecstasy . . . The amount of drugs and alcohol that I was taking when we were together, I almost pushed myself over the edge.

That's the thing about drugs . . . I thought I was having a good time but I was just totally numbing myself. And when your brain is toxic, everything is tainted. It becomes too violent too quickly—*emotionally* violent. It was like sitting in a storm. Even sex was tainted. We were toxifying our passions so it turned into this bad spiral. Really intense, really hard-core. Maybe it was like 2 percent warmth. That's probably what I liked best, those moments.

Passion? I know it's overrated. That adrenaline rush, it's not real. Whenever you're living in passion, you're living in the fear that you're going to lose something. And if you live in that fear all the time, you're not acting out of your heart. You start acting out of who you think you should be instead of who you are. I get off so much more on the feeling of love. It's just so much more full-bodied and heartwarming.

With him, though, I was living with so much fear that I was totally disconnected from myself. I wasn't following my heart. That's why I never had a child with him. I knew it in my bones, but my mind was telling me, "I'm going to make it work." But a bad relationship—*passionate* relationships like that—can drive you to the grave.

Jealousy turns me off entirely. Any type of jealousy or anger. The man that I'm with now, he had severe anger and jealousy issues. Whenever my eyes would go off he would accuse me of thinking of my ex: "Are you thinking about him?" An anonymous text would come in, I'd look at the phone, and he was like, "Is it him?" Just paranoid. So I immediately told him, "You have to work on yourself. I'm going to help you, we're going to do it together, but I can't live with a man that's accusing me of things that I didn't do."

The key is, when you're in a relationship, you really have to learn how to talk to each other, to listen to each other. To *dialogue*. But what often happens is that you say something, the other person reacts, and then you start having an argument that has nothing to do with the real reason why you were complaining in the first place. Because you're only listening to yourself, you're not really listening to what the other person is saying back to you.

In my relationship now we still have moments like that where it feels like a precipice, where you're sitting there looking off and you're just like, "This is finished. This has gone too far." That's why I think marriage is good because it really gives you the extra commitment to that person and to yourself. Too many couples are giving up too quickly. *I don't like you because you did that, I'm going to leave and go get somebody else.* They just decide to throw in the towel. It's like disposable relationships. Now, with my boyfriend, if something isn't working, I immediately put it on the table so we can talk about it, even if it's like putting a needle in an abscess. You *have* to.

Women, I think, are very good at not saying something and then resenting and that's when you do foolish things. That resentment turns into anger and then before you know it, you create a rift in the relationship and you go off and get drunk and you cheat. I don't believe you can live in a relationship and cheat. I don't believe in relationships where the man is having an affair but he still loves his wife. It's like several actors playing the same role in a film. It's very dangerous. It's so unhappy.

I think if you stop having sex it's not because you don't desire it, it's because it's not working with your partner. I think sex is the most important part of a relationship. That physical desire to be with somebody, to share your body with somebody, to feel comfortable with somebody. And if you're not feeling comfortable with yourself then you have to take care of that. You have to stay attractive, you can't become Two-Ton Tully. Even after twenty years of marriage you have to keep that look in your eyes. Because when you feel unhappy and unwanted, and he feels unhappy and unwanted, that's when you go off and have an affair.

I don't necessarily think that male affairs are less emotionally involved; I've certainly had a lot of affairs that were purely sexual. But I do think men are more kinky, more voyeuristic, they live in fantasy more. That's why women aren't going out to the strip club. My ex-husband actually liked porno flicks. But he liked the ones that had transvestites in them, which I think twice about today. Maybe he's bisexual, I don't know. But at the time I was worried that it was *me*. That's another thing: You always think the problem is *you*. I thought maybe there was something wrong with me that I didn't like that stuff. He'd say, "What's the difference? It *looks* like a woman." And I'd say, "But that woman has a cock!"

I think it all has to do with trying to get away from the whole image of the mother. Separating from that desire. Trying to find fifty thousand different ways of acting out things just to separate that bond. That's why you have to be careful with what your man is fantasizing about. You can't ignore it; you can't just turn the station. Even if it annoys you to get dressed up sometimes, you have to do it. You have to explore the fantasies. Because if you don't, they're just going to be played out somewhere else.

"Jealousy is an illusion. It's there if you want it to be."

ALIAS: Steve

OCCUPATION: Lawyer

DATE OF BIRTH: 1974

CURRENT MARRIAGE STATUS: Married

DO YOU HAVE ANY CHILDREN? Two (with my current wife)

WHERE YOU GREW UP: Louisiana

WHERE YOU LIVE: Louisiana

YEAR OF MARRIAGE: 2003, 2006

HOW LONG YOU DATED BEFORE YOU WERE MARRIED: Two years;
    a year and a half

YEAR OF DIVORCE: 2005

I remember being at a friend's wedding, and before the ceremony, all the old men got together with the groom to give him some advice. They basically said to just give in and you will be fine. There were no tales of triumph and lifelong passion. The old-timers basically gave the same advice as if you were about to endure a week in the forest. *Respect Mother Nature, try not to use too much energy, and do whatever you can to survive.*

My parents have been married since the late '60s. Growing up, I was always aware of the fighting and just thought that they hated each other. It wasn't until I was older—when their marriage was tested by tragedy—that I realized what they really had.

I was about two years into my marriage with my ex. My little brother, who was twenty-five at the time, had been struggling with pills and cocaine. The day before his twenty-sixth birthday, the family planned to take him to a steak house. I hadn't spoken to him that day, only the day before. I sensed something in his voice and asked if he was being good, not doing anything he shouldn't. He assured me that he hadn't touched any bad stuff and I told him that I'd see him tomorrow.

The next day, no one heard from him. Eventually, my father went and used his key to get into my brother's apartment and found him in bed. We all knew what had happened.

My parents got closer and more supportive of each other—their commitment never wavered. But my marriage went the opposite way. The support I got from my ex was short-lived and transparent. It was almost as though the attention had been taken away from her for too long. There was, of course, compassion that my brother had died, but it diminished by the day.

I realized that the marriage was bullshit six months later, when I started fighting with my older brother. He accused me of things—like being a bad influence. As our relationship slowly came to an end, my ex just didn't really care. She said, "Fuck him," and told me not to speak to him. Period. I remember saying, "But he's the only brother I have left." Her response, "*Waah waah*—people die, get over it."

Everyone's spouse changes after the wedding. Women always do. From the way they dress to the way they tolerate the things that make you who you are. Like a game of poker, you don't get to see the entire hand until most of the time it's too late. My ex showed only her high cards at the beginning—all smiles and sexy underwear. By the end, she had visible frown lines and granny panties.

I know very few people who say they are the same person they were before they got married. There is always someone who gives up a lot. Most often, the guys get the shaft and have to become whoever they need to become just to minimize the aggravation and pestering. For me, my sense of self withered by the day. Freedom was sacrificed—time with friends, mostly my female friends. So I just began to expect less out of life. It was like voluntarily checking into prison. Every time I spoke to an old friend, if it was a girl, I'd get questioned. *Did you fuck her? Did you ever kiss her?* And even with something like golf, *Why do you have to play twice a week? Isn't once a week enough?* Everything needed an explanation.

I can almost mark the point where the relationship started going downhill—it was really when the trust was broken, a few months into the marriage. It was my fault, but at the same time it was something that was pretty stupid. E-mails.

After you get married, for the most part, you lose that boost to your ego that some healthy flirtation with a woman would provide. You rely on your spouse for that boost, but it's not quite the same thing. Either she doesn't give it or eventually it becomes like when your mother gives you a compliment. Of course she has to say that you're the best or the brightest.

So one day when the wife was away, I e-mailed an old friend from college. A girl. She was someone that I had never had a relationship with, but after college, we made out a few times, mostly after sharing a bottle of Jack Daniel's. So one night I e-mailed her and she happened to be online. We were joking around and I told her that the wife was away and that she should "come on by for a little somethin' somethin'." It was a joke—I was just fishing for a somewhat stimulating response, that was it.

The only problem was that about a month later, my wife thought it was her right to snoop through my e-mails. The truth is, it was harmless—but I'm sure she never quite believed me.

I don't know what the real definition of romance is. As a husband, I was "romantic" in that I knew what plans to make for special occasions, brought flowers home, bought gifts, jewelry, and cards, and planned nice vacations. But I wouldn't say I was romantic, because I did those things just so she would be somewhat happy and nice and hopefully give me some sex.

People talk about dead-end jobs but I think a dead-end sex life is just as bad. Sex is the most important thing. Sex can defuse a bad situation, sex can aid in reconciliation, sex can rid you of the stress of the day. A lack of sex just makes everything worse. I married a girl who for some reason was never into giving head. I became one of those guys who basically had to ask for a blow job on his birthday and only got to come in her mouth on our honeymoon. She let me fuck her in the ass once, at the beginning, I'm not sure if it was out of obligation or what.

I was always the one who initiated sex. There was limited fantasy, no dress-up or shit like that, and it all just got boring—same position, same routine, like clockwork. There were times she would let me pop in a porn but that got old, too. In retrospect, the sex was fucking pathetic but it was like I was brainwashed to think it was okay.

Men are more likely to pay for sex because men are more likely deprived of it. Women do not understand that if they deny their husbands sex, they will get it somewhere else. Women use it as a weapon and have no idea how many men have paid for sex or had one-nighters, whether it's a hand job at a strip club, a call girl, or even a drunk girl at a bar. If they truly knew the percentages, at least among people I know, they would be astounded to the point where even the Girl Scouts would teach that a woman's duty is to make sure her husband is completely drained of all cum before he leaves the house.

Interestingly, the happiest couples I've seen, with the strongest marriages, were the swingers I met with my now wife on our trip to Hedonism in Jamaica. They knew exactly what life and marriage was about. It wasn't about unnatural boundaries or restrictions. It was about a mutual understanding of what pleasure and commitment was. It really did open my eyes. While we may not have jumped into their beds, it was fun to live a bit more freely. And one thing they didn't have at Hedonism is jealousy. There was nothing to be jealous about. What that tells me is that jealousy is an illusion. It's there if you want it to be.

I got married the first time because I think I was in love with the idea of it. But we fought right off the bat, and even called off the engagement at one point. The early warning sign was that when we fought, it wasn't just a fight. Someone always said it was over, or "get the fuck out," or "don't call me again." Fights were never productive, only destructive. It's been so different with my wife now. When we're in a fight, I can look at her and say to myself, she is still beautiful. It's like she gave me back my faith in women.

My advice for someone getting married would not be to learn how to get along, but to learn how to fight fairly and productively. Now my wife and I have a signal and know how to end a fight. Regardless of whether anything has been resolved, we can snap out of our bad moods and move on by holding up our index finger and signaling to the other to do the same. We count "one, two, three," and snap our fingers. The fight is over. The rule is that we can never refuse to snap, and so far that has worked. It's like a safety valve to defuse any situation and prevent a fight from ruining our day. It works by e-mail and text message as well.

"The biggest mistake a man can make in bed is having a lack of enthusiasm. And I think the biggest mistake a woman can make is also a lack of enthusiasm. Sex is a team sport. It should be a lot of fucking fun."

ALIAS: Sloan

OCCUPATION: Engineer

YEAR OF BIRTH: 1979

CURRENT MARRIAGE STATUS: Single

DO YOU HAVE ANY CHILDREN? No

WHERE YOU GREW UP: Nevada

WHERE YOU LIVE: New York

YEAR OF MARRIAGE: 1999

HOW LONG YOU DATED BEFORE YOU WERE MARRIED: Two years

YEAR OF DIVORCE: Separated 2002; officially divorced 2004

When did you start falling in love with your boss?
I think it was probably my second or third day at the office. I worked at an architecture firm. He was six years older than me, very handsome, really talented. He just came up to me and said, "Sloan, would you like to go to dinner with me?" And I was just like, "Is it a date?" And he was like, "Yeah, I'd like it to be."

Did you kiss that night?
Yeah. I went home with him, the whole nine yards. And then I just never really left. I was there for weeks on end and then I moved in. We got engaged after three months. He just immediately brought me into his world. There was never any hesitancy on his part, like, "Is she the one?" It was this total whirlwind fairy-tale scenario.

Was his certainty contagious?
Oh yeah. Any kind of positive anything is contagious, that kind

of enthusiasm. And as a woman it's always flattering to have somebody like you for the right reasons.

What are the wrong reasons?
You don't want to be liked for the "on paper" reasons, whatever those boring reasons are.

How did you find out he was cheating on you?
He was on a business trip and he called me because his e-mail wasn't working. So he asked me, "Can you log in to my account? I need you to forward this e-mail." I was like, "Yeah, what is it?" He doesn't organize his e-mails so I just started scrolling through and I saw all these messages from different girls. It was right after Valentine's Day. "Thanks for the roses!" "Good morning!" It was all there. Everything. I was just like, okay—*wow*. I didn't see that coming. I mean, he was the guy that I never thought would cheat on me.

Why?
He was just so glossy in love with me. I could never do anything wrong. Like, when we'd go shopping—when we'd go *anywhere*—he'd carry my purse. He just doted on me. He treated me with such respect. Well, in theory.

How did you confront him about the e-mails?
He got back from his trip and I was just like, "Okay, we need to talk. What's going on?" He tried to deny everything, but it was like, "No, no, no. It's not a question of *are* you doing it. I *know* you're doing it—I have all their e-mails—and I responded to some of them, too [laughs]. So what do you want to do about it?"

It sounds as if you were very cavalier about it. Were you jealous?
It wasn't so much that I was jealous, but I felt really betrayed. It was just like, "Why couldn't you have just *talked* to me about

this?" That's the real question. Do you have the sort of relationship where you can be honest enough about what you need and what you're doing? If you can have those conversations before you start being self-destructive, it can salvage everything. But the second it becomes deceitful, that's a red flag.

Did you attempt to salvage your marriage even though he was being deceitful?
Yes. I calmed down and he was like, "Listen, I love you. I don't want to break up. I don't want to lose you." So I asked him, "Do you want to try an open relationship?" And he was like, "Really? Oh, that'd be great." And it was like, "Okay, let's try it. What are the parameters going to be?" Initially it was that we couldn't have people in the same city. It was more for when we traveled. At that point, I was going to Chicago all the time and he was going to LA.

And you were honestly okay with all this?
I'm very open-minded. So we started doing it. And you know what happened? We never had sex again. *Ever.* We became like best friends. And when I say "best friends"—we were *best friends*. I'd call him and be like, "I just had a date with this guy. I really like him. What do you think I should wear?"

When did you decide to get divorced?
I was on a business trip in Michigan and I flew back and I just totally lost it on the airplane. I just knew I had to leave him. So I went home and he was already in bed. Then we woke up the next morning and he looked at me and said, "Wow, you don't love me anymore." He knew instantly. And I was like, "No, it's not that." And he was like, "When do you want to move out?" And I moved out the next week.

Were you still attracted to him?
No. When I'm done, I'm done.

A lot of people say that communication and compromise are the most important things in a marriage. But there's another "C" word that's been coming up a lot. "Criticism." How do you express the things you don't like about the other person in a way that isn't hurtful? How do you keep the criticism constructive?

You have to talk openly and give some sense of reality. Like, I don't need this watered-down version.

Right, but how do you do that?

Hypercommunication. And a real sense of compassion for the other person.

What about sexual communication?

That's essential, too.

Do you think men are lustier than women?

Yeah, probably. But women are at a very interesting point right now. It's not that we've never had the same sex drive as men, it's just that the cultural parameters have prohibited us from engaging in that kind of behavior. I think men are more open because they're allowed to be. It's okay for a man to be dirty and horny and say all sorts of things, but when a girl says something like that, it's like, "Oh, my God!"

Why do you think men make such stupid decisions when they're thinking with "the little head"?

It's biological. Their penises short-wire their brains. It just shuts off.

Is that a fact?

I think it is [laughs]. I mean, I can't cite any scientific facts right now, but speaking from personal experience, I'm pretty sure it's true. I'm always floored at what men are willing to risk to get into your pants. It's just like, *Whoa.*

Have you ever had an affair with a married man?
Yes. For some reason I'm like a married man magnet. That's a whole interesting role to explore—the mistress. You see how hungry these men are for even the littlest things. Like someone asking them how their day was, just paying attention to them.

What else did you learn about men by being a mistress?
All men cheat. At some point or another. Given the opportunity, they will. It doesn't necessarily mean that he loves his wife any less. Their penises are just designed to do it. It's a very carnal thing.

And as a wife, you'd be understanding of that behavior?
I'm *encouraging* of that type of behavior. Again, as long as you're honest about it. But I haven't had a monogamous relationship since I was twenty-three. That's kind of scary to think about. I don't even know what that looks like anymore.

Do a lot of your friends talk to you about their sex lives?
Yeah. I have two sets of friends—my new, younger friends, and all my friends that got married and had kids—and they're just leading totally different lives. None of my married friends want to take responsibility for it. They just turn off and they're like, "Yeah, we're not having sex anymore." And it's like, "Okay, what are you doing to fix that? What are you walking around the house in? Are you making any advances?" I don't know what goes through their heads. Just because you're married doesn't mean you still don't have to seduce and flirt and have sexual energy going around. Of course you have to! *Especially* when you're working and doing the kid thing.

A lot of the men whom I interviewed complained that their wives never gave blow jobs. It really seemed to hurt their feelings. What do you think about that?

My first thought is "What's wrong with these women?" And then I remember that I used to be one of them. I never put a penis in my mouth until I was twenty-four. Which means that my ex-husband never got a blow job. Oddly enough, he never complained or pushed it. When I finally decided to try it, I knew that it was going to be a deep, dark rabbit hole for me.

Why?

Because I love a man coming in my mouth.

Do you?

I'm actually kind of obsessed with men and their cum.

Do many of your friends feel the same way?

I never gave it much thought and just assumed that all women swallowed until a few months ago. I was having brunch with some newer girlfriends (my age) and the topic turned to sex, of course, and then to blow jobs, and it came out that none of them swallowed. One had tried it and the rest of them wouldn't dare. Some of them were worried about the taste. I told them, "Just give him pineapple juice the night before. And if you really want to avoid tasting it as much as possible, then make sure he's in the back of your throat when he comes. Don't let it pool in your mouth."

Is there a female equivalent to swallowing? Something slightly transgressive or "dirty" that women want guys to do?

I don't know if there's a female equivalent, but I do have a gold standard way of evaluating men. If they go down on me when I'm having my period, that's just pretty awesome. But it has to be their idea. And they have to do it enthusiastically, like it's the most exciting thing that has ever happened.

What's the biggest mistake that guys make in bed?
I think the biggest mistake a man can make in bed is having a lack of enthusiasm. And I think the biggest mistake a woman can make is also a lack of enthusiasm. Sex is a team sport. It should be a lot of fucking fun.

ENGAGING THE ELEPHANTS

All married couples should learn the art of battle
as they should learn the art of making love. Good battle is
objective and honest—never vicious or cruel.
—Ann Landers

When we ask for advice,
we are usually looking for an accomplice.
—Saul Bellow

As soon as I saw the elephant I knew with perfect certainty
that I ought not to shoot him.
—George Orwell

My grandpa's Valentine's Day card said, "Hearts speak when words cannot." But if I've learned anything from my five failed relationships, it's that hearts don't speak—they murmur. We're verbal creatures; we need to talk.

We need to talk about the elephants.

Unlike my grandpa and me, these thick-skinned giants are masters of communication, able to send and receive messages over great distances using subsonic rumblings. They're not shy about PDA, hugging out in the open by intertwining their trunks, and they can recognize themselves in a mirror, leading scientists to believe that they're "self-aware" enough to experience complex emotions such as empathy and altruism. They even bury their dead.

Mighty Mary was an Asian elephant billed as "the largest living land animal on earth"—three inches taller than Jumbo, P. T. Barnum's prized pachyderm. Able to pitch baseballs and to "play twenty-five tunes on the musical horns," she was the five-ton pride of Charlie Sparks's World Famous Show, a struggling traveling circus that rolled through the South with just ten railroad cars, compared to Barnum's eighty-nine. Hoping to get a leg up on his competition, Sparks targeted the Bible-thumping crowd, touting his spiritual superiority, claiming that his was the only "100 percent Sunday School Circus: Moral, entertaining, and instructive!" Tragically, the cunning showman earned a place in big top history only by presiding over the infamously *im*moral act of hanging Mary by the neck in front of a crowd that, by design, included most of the children from the local Sunday school.

Here's what happened. In September 1916, in Kingsport, Tennessee, a copper-topped wrangler named Walter "Red" Eldridge was told to take Mary to a nearby watering hole so she could splash around and cool off. On their way, she saw a watermelon rind in the dirt and bent down for a bite. That's when Red made the fatal mistake of scolding her, prodding her behind the ear with a bullhook. He must have poked a little too hard because Mary whipped around, snatched him up in her trunk, and slammed him to the ground, killing him instantly. Then, as if posing for a victory picture, she put her foot on his head, squashing it like, well, a melon.

Word of Red's "murder" spread quickly, and the townsfolk cried for frontier justice: "Kill the elephant! Kill the elephant!" The papers took to calling her Murderous Mary, and nobody in the surrounding areas was about to invite this rogue beast to entertain their families. So Sparks did what any other soulless barker would have done. He gave the people what they wanted. He turned the calamity into a spectacle.

On September 13, 1916, in front of twenty-five hundred paying customers, Sparks led the thirty-year-old elephant to a makeshift gallows that he'd erected at the Clinchfield Railroad Yards in Erwin, Tennessee. Mary was to be hanged by a chain from an industrial derrick used for hauling lumber from freight cars. On first try, the chain snapped, crashing Mary to the ground, shattering her hip. As she wailed in pain, Sparks calmed the crowd and went looking for a thicker noose. The winch was put in motion once again, and this time Mary died.

Sparks let her swing there for half an hour and then buried her in an unmarked pit by the train tracks. But little did he know, when Mary hit the ground, she woke the dead. And ever since, the ghosts of these benevolent behemoths have been haunting us, taunting us, squatting in our rooms like ticking time bombs, daring us to look them in the eye.

It's Murderous Mary's revenge.

Indeed, the elephant in the room is the most dangerous breed of all, responsible for wrecking more homes than any other domestic menace. Too big to hide, they're easy to spot but impossible to kill. They feed off human avoidance, growing larger and more violent the longer they're ignored, spreading uncertainty and anxiety like rats spread disease. And they're prolific breeders.

In my last relationship, my girlfriend and I lived together in a Brooklyn brownstone but it felt like we were camping in the African bush. We were surrounded. They were in our bedroom as we slept back to back, in our kitchen when we'd say, "I don't care, whatever you wanna eat is fine." They even followed us onto the subway, where we wouldn't hold hands. It was my fault; I had this whole excuse about how PDA makes lonely people feel lonelier, so I didn't want to flaunt our togetherness. The truth is, holding hands made me feel like a fraud because we were never really together. I could feel it in our grip: too tight, not tight enough. The key, said a man from New York, is to "hold on loosely." But we were never able to do that.

It was oddly comforting to find out that everyone I interviewed has dealt with an elephant situation. Or worse: They *didn't* deal with it. We talked about the cycles of withdrawal and withholding, the dangers of delusion, how optimism can lead to inertia, and how you can't be present if you're living in the future. I've done that plenty of times, hoped the bad stuff would just go away, justifying my avoidance with high-minded maxims like "Ask not for what ought to be offered" and thinking, "It'll get better, it'll get better."

Fortunately, everybody agreed on a seemingly simple solution: *Engage the elephants,* whether they're about kissing, money, in-laws, or whatever. Indeed, the only way to mollify them is to acknowledge their existence—to talk about them openly—before it's too late. It sounds easy, but for some reason it can be more difficult than hanging them from a derrick.

"Yes, I saw her e-mail because I was able to get her passwords through key logging software I added to the computer," says Adam. "I had no idea that my wife liked to do all that stuff."

"He refused to acknowledge that he was having any issues," says Sharon. "So things just kept getting worse and worse."

"I felt lonely, but couldn't identify it as loneliness," says Nicole. "How could I be lonely married to the love of my life?"

At various points during each of my five failed relationships, I've thought that I was with "the love of my life." Could those relationships have worked out if I was a better engager? I called three of my exes to ask:

Apparently I "can keep a pretty safe distance." I'm "an eloquent listener" but I can "hold a grudge with both hands" and at times I "can be *too* direct, a little rough." I'm living too much in my head, not enough in my heart, and I "have a sense of entitlement when it comes to relationships, an expectation of perfection in other people"—and in myself—that can lead to "disappointment" and "withdrawal." When I asked them explicitly if we did a good job of engaging the elephants, they all said the same thing: *not really.*

At least now I know for certain. You can tiptoe around them, buy a last-minute Valentine's Day card, and hope that they'll wander off on their own. But the elephants in the room aren't going anywhere until they've prodded us to do our penance by coming clean and putting everything on the table.

So I've made a new rule in their honor. The next time I'm feeling like part of "that sad couple" in the restaurant, sitting through one of those interminable, small-talky meals, I'm going to break the tension with a toast: "To Mighty Mary." And then start talking big.

" 'If it's not a secret, it's a whole different level; he's not hiding it from you, he's trying to work it out with you.' "

ALIAS: Diane

OCCUPATION: Teacher

YEAR OF BIRTH: 1946

CURRENT MARRIAGE STATUS: Single

DO YOU HAVE ANY CHILDREN? Yes. Two children, thirty-four and
    thirty-seven

WHERE YOU GREW UP: New York

WHERE YOU LIVE: Connecticut

YEAR OF MARRIAGE: 1975

HOW LONG YOU DATED BEFORE YOU WERE MARRIED: One year

YEAR OF DIVORCE: 2001

How did he propose? Well, we were dating, and we had a fight. He had given me a gold bangle bracelet and then he said something, I don't remember what, but it wasn't very nice. And then I said, "Well, take the bracelet back, then!" And he just squashed it in his hands and said, "I was going to ask you to marry me." And I said, "*Marry* you? I didn't even think you *liked* me!"

The book I was gonna write was called *How Come Everybody Loves My Husband Except Me?* I mean, there were lots of things that should've been red flags. He was wonderful and charming—he *still* is—but he was very difficult, he had a temper. At some point I thought, "Maybe he's a little manic-depressive, but artists are." I guess now you might say it's "bipolar." But at the time I found it all to be, "Gee, this is interesting, this is a challenge."

He was very clever, very funny, very talented—unlike anybody I had ever known. I grew up in a house in the Bronx with a backyard and a front porch and plenty of games out in the street. I had twenty-one first cousins, all living within fifteen minutes of me. I had been going out with regular people from the neighborhood, or that I'd met at Queens College. The boyfriend I had on and off at the time was going to be an accountant. Very sweet, but I would shrug my shoulders and say, "Do I really want to live in his mother's house in the Bronx?"

My husband, well, he had gone to school in California, where he was a stock car racing champion. Guys I grew up with weren't racing champions! But here was this *artist*. He was a photographer. He had a little MG. He didn't own a suit. He lived in Manhattan and his family had a house in the Hamptons. He was tall and I thought he was very sexy in a different kind of way. I'd look at him and just think he was so cute even though other people didn't see that.

My father was very talented—very good with his hands, could build anything, could fix anything—and my husband was very much like that, too. He was the first man I met who could do all of those things. So yeah, I did see a little bit of my father in him, and that was attractive. And he became as successful as he could possibly be. He was working for one of the biggest magazines in the country. We traveled a lot and he would get stopped at the airport going through customs because people would recognize his name.

He also got involved in politics—he was the mayor where our summer home was. It was a smaller community, but he ran for office and he was elected. And he appointed himself as the police chief *and* the fire chief. Mayors appoint those positions [laughs]. And I was really giving him a hard time because the firemen were all volunteers. They worked so hard, they went to school, and now here's this guy who knows nothing who's going to tell them all what to do?

It wasn't the ambition that was a turnoff, it was the neglect of other things I thought were important. I think ambition can be internal—you set a goal and you strive to meet it and it doesn't matter whether the rest of the world is patting you on the back. But egotism implies getting rewards *outside* yourself. You can be ambitious, but you can still say, "I haven't really spent any time with the kids at the beach." You can do both. But his ego was just beyond that. I've told my daughters not to marry anybody that's going to push them out of the way when they're blocking the mirror. You don't want a man who thinks he's better looking than you are!

Of course, when I wasn't mad at him, I really loved him. But I just couldn't understand why he would explode, yelling and screaming about how his life was terrible and how God was punishing him. Like, there was somebody that I worked with that he didn't like, and he was *furious* that I didn't dislike this other person, also. You know, if somebody was on his shit list, they had to be on mine, too. Or even little things like . . . I never, ever got headaches. But one night we were supposed to go someplace and I had this really horrendous headache and I just didn't feel like going out. And he'd just blow up because I was ruining his evening.

There were many times over the years when I'd say to myself: "Gee, I can't stand him, but what am I going to do? Where am I going to go? I don't work. I'm old. I really love my kids, I like who I am in my life, and he makes it all possible. I can't walk away from this." So I kind of hung in there and I kept trying to make it better. But I would get really upset because I just couldn't believe that God was somehow punishing him when everything seemed so nice. I just couldn't believe that we were supposed to be so much in love and yet here was this person who was so unhappy so often and who saw very little good or happiness in the world. And I'm quite a Pollyanna so it was very tough for me. But I hung in there for twenty-six years.

My husband was never my best friend because anything that wasn't good news—anything that was an issue—was going to ruin his day. We would talk about stuff but he wasn't somebody who talked much. No sitting up in bed and talking for hours and hours. He felt that he was a very good husband and father if he was providing. And that was certainly something from the generation before—you went to work and you came home, and as long as you had the money to pay for the food in the house, that was your only job.

Now, in terms of evolution, a little history. Man was not, by necessity, somebody who was going to talk a lot. The man was the hunter. So they'd go out, and even though there might be a few of them, they couldn't talk. They had to sneak up on the animals, so there couldn't be any conversation. Meanwhile, the women were sitting around the fire, doing the corn, the children, the caring. And so I think it's still somewhat because of that, that men are not programmed—not conditioned—to search out that kind of companionship. I mean, I have many women friends and I think it's fairly obvious that men have very few friends.

Sex? We had lots of sex but there was very little lovemaking. What's the difference? Sex is, "What do you mean, you're tired? I'm not tired. I've gotta do this now." And I'd say, "Okay, do whatever you need to do, just put me back when you're done." As opposed to a nice conversation, something other than, "Okay, I'm turning off the TV now."

There was infidelity, but it was something that was fairly brief. And when it was happening, he told me all about it. He had been at a meeting at a bar and he met somebody there, and she told him how funny he was, how handsome he was, how nice he was, what a great guy he was. And he thought, "This is nice to hear— as opposed to dealing with teenagers at home."

So we did do a little counseling and I came out of it thinking, "Of course he should've said, 'No,' and he should've walked away from it." But the books I'd read said, "If it's not a secret, it's a whole different level; he's not hiding it from you, he's trying to work it out with you." And so he definitely always felt tremendously guilty, but I said, "This is not worth ending a marriage over. I'll end it for other things, but not because he came across someone who made him feel like a god."

* * *

If I had to list what I was looking for in someone, it would be intelligence, compassion, a sense of humor, and some charm. I like charm. Another very important thing is passion, and not physical passion necessarily, but passion about life, about what he's interested in. But people have very different priorities at twenty-five than they do at fifty.

I think the fear of being alone is gone now because there are so many people who have ended their marriages and are surviving. The Internet is great for that because you're seeing your peers, your coworkers, and they're all okay, they're taking care of themselves, they're able to function. Whereas twenty or thirty years ago, you didn't see that. You saw people in total breakdowns if they were divorced.

Internet dating, that's the whole social world now. I mean, here I am in my bedroom and I could be writing sexy notes to twenty different people. I almost feel like I should be dressed nicely when I'm looking at people's profiles or answering their letters. But they don't know I'm lying here in my fuzzy bathrobe and my big red slippers!

"If it happens more than once, get out. *Go.* There's no place for violence in a marriage. In *any* relationship."

ALIAS: Sharon

OCCUPATION: In between jobs

YEAR OF BIRTH: 1982

CURRENT MARRIAGE STATUS: Divorced

DO YOU HAVE ANY CHILDREN? No

WHERE YOU GREW UP: Montana

WHERE YOU LIVE: In transit

YEAR OF MARRIAGE: 2006

HOW LONG YOU DATED BEFORE YOU WERE MARRIED: We dated for
  a few years ages seventeen to nineteen off and on, then dated for about five
  months before we were married

YEAR OF DIVORCE: Pending

I remember the first words Billy said to me. I was seventeen years old, we were at this party in Billings, Montana, and he offered me some pistachios. And I was so nervous that I just said, "No." Even though I *love* pistachios! I was just really shy and weird that night because I'd just gotten out of this crazy boarding school.

I went to a very expensive, highly restrictive emotional growth boarding school in northern Idaho. It was a CEDU school. Totally messed up. There are support groups for it now. We had to do these things called *propheets,* where you'd go through two or three days of being sleep-deprived, and they'd feed you very little, and they'd shove all this weird propaganda down your throat, asking really hard questions about your childhood. They'd totally break you down. Then they'd give you this pillow, and you had to take another pillow and *beat* that pillow and do what's called "running your shit." *Getting the anger out.* And they're playing John Lennon music so everyone's crying and yelling and beating their pillows!

If you didn't do it, they'd put you on a restriction. They were called "bans." They would put you on bans from smiling, bans from laughing. Yes—*bans on smiling*. They'd be like, "What are you doing smiling? You're on bans!" If you were banned from talking to anyone, and you talked, they would isolate you, they would lock you in this room all day by yourself. Or you'd need to go on work assignment, hard labor, like you'd have to work in the woodshed sawing wood. Or they'd be like, "We're going to put you out in a field far away and make you dig up rocks all day." I got that *a lot* [laughs].

People are still seriously messed up over it. I mean, the worst punishment you could give a fifteen-year-old is to isolate them and not let them smile or talk to anyone. That's just so destructive in every way. I went there for two years, from fifteen to seventeen, and when I got out, I did not know how to function. There were some lawsuits—a lot of kids killed themselves. I'm sure those parents were like, "Um, I sent my child to an emotional growth boarding school and when he came out he killed himself. Obviously he didn't really grow emotionally."

This is so bad, but my mom would always say, "All men are exactly the same, they all want the same thing, so you might as well marry a rich one." And I was like, "Good job, Mom—you're on doctor number two!"

I grew up in a really nice three-story house with an indoor swimming pool. Very religious—Episcopalian. Youth group and all that. I *hated* it. My mom took anything in our house that had a devil on it, or a dragon, or anything associated with magic or the mythical, and she burned it all because she thought it was evil. My dad was a doctor, an oncologist. He had an affair when my mom was pregnant with me and they divorced when I was six months old. It always seemed so hypocritical—my dad was singing in the church choir and having an affair. I'm like, "Hello? What are we doing here?"

When I met Billy, I remember thinking that he was so different from the guys that I'd grown up with. He definitely wasn't conventionally attractive. An Abercrombie model, most people are like, "That is a sexy man." But to me, that's like eating at Applebee's. I mean, yeah, it's good, but it's so generic. I'd rather eat some kind of fusion food or at a backdoor mom-and-pop restaurant, y'know?

Billy was a year older, he was eighteen, and he was living on his own, had his own house, drove a really cool Chevy Blazer. He was working in the methane fields as a roustabout. He was just so talented, he could do anything. He'd be like, "You need a fence built? No problem, I'll build it next weekend." His dad was a miner in the coal fields and his mom is part Native American so she's very much a country woman. Like *skin the deer and cook it for dinner*—that kind of thing. I'm not like that at all. I'm like, "I'll skin the tofu!" And so I think she kind of saw me as a little bit snobby.

He proposed over Christmas. We were both living in California at the time. I was going to school in Santa Cruz and he had joined the marines and was stationed nearby. We were home visiting our families in Montana, and he got a little ring, borrowed his mom's truck, and drove me out to the canyon and showed me a bench he carved out of a log. And I thought he was going to say, "Will you marry me?" or something romantic. But he didn't. He was like, "Be my wife." And it was sweet but I was kind of like, "Really? That's all you came up with? That was kind of lame."

When we were young, when we first started dating, we went to a movie at the local movie theater, and he jokingly said something about me being his girlfriend. And I was like, "Oh, am I your girlfriend?"

And he was like, "I thought so."

And I was like, "Well, you never asked me."

So he goes, "Oh, well, will you be my girlfriend?" You know, like, all retardedly [laughs].

And I was like, "Not if you ask like that. You need to wait a week and ask me again, seriously."

A week later—to the day, almost to the minute on the clock—we were at his house, and he gets down on one knee, and he goes, "Sharon, will you be my girlfriend?" And I said, "Yes, I will!" That was way more romantic than when he asked me to marry him.

Yes, I can be very difficult and pouty when I'm let down, and I think that can be hard on people. It's probably a flaw of mine that I have these super-romantic expectations—disgustingly so. I really have this need to keep things magical. And I think maybe it can get to the point where people are like, "Fuck, Sharon, we've had five magical nights this week, can we just go to Burger King?"

We were married in October, he deployed in January. It all happened very fast. I was twenty-four years old and very naive about the whole thing. Living in a military environment. Military wives, the military base. I thought, "He'll do his job, he'll be fine, he'll come home, we'll move on." I thought, "Yeah, he'll have some issues, but he'll be okay." We talked about it before he left, like, "If you come back and you need help or you need therapy, you'll get it, right?" And he said, "Yeah, if I need it, I'll get it."

His unit—a unit is thirteen guys—was sent to this crazy part of Afghanistan where nobody had been. They were the first guys to push into it, so there was nothing there. No base. No camp. Nobody had patrolled the area, nobody knew the surrounding towns. It was all new. They found an old castle to set up in. I think they were hit for the first time in early March. That's when it became real to me.

They lost three guys. I knew these guys, I knew their girlfriends, I knew their wives. And one of the guys was super young, his wife was nineteen, and it was just like, "Oh, my God." Like, *whoa*. I was totally freaked out. I'm going to get emotional talking about it. Another guy, he was married and he survived, but he was burned. Like horribly, horribly burned. And his wife was like . . . [she tears up]. I mean, they were so in love, and he was just . . . By the end of the tour, out of thirteen guys, they were down to five. It was insane.

Billy came home in September and we were so happy to see each other. But it was so emotional because the guys that were injured were there, too. The guy that was burned, they had to amputate his hands. What happened was, there were four guys in the Humvee when it blew up. Three of them were badly burned, but escaped. One of them was pinned down. They couldn't get him out—it was too hot. They couldn't save him. They watched him burn alive. So they were carrying around all this guilt. And it's just like, "Nobody expects you to run into a burning vehicle, you did everything that you could." But I don't know how anyone gets over that. *Ever.*

It's crazy, the Marine Corps brings these guys back from this insane eight-month tour in a war zone in Afghanistan and they're just like, "See ya, back to your real life, go be with your wives, go play with your two-year-old." There's no therapy. No "Let's talk about what happened." *Nothing.* And there's no encouragement to seek it out—it's actually the opposite. Because if you do, you won't be promoted, you won't get a raise. They're not promoting anybody with psychological issues, y'know? Even among the guys, it's looked down on. One of the guys in Billy's unit went to talk to a therapist and they were all like, "That's so weak." Even the wives were like, "What's wrong with him?" And it's like, *What?* Go look up post-traumatic stress disorder. There's nothing "wrong" with him—these guys need help!

Billy was totally freaked out when he got back, like if someone closed a car door, he would immediately hit the ground. It was like a bomb went off. Fourth of July was crazy, all the explosions. Because his body was still operating on extreme distress mode. *Where's it coming from? What's the situation? Where's my gun?* He needed to have his gun with him at all times, which was terrifying. We went on a trip to San Francisco and he had his gun in the side of the door and I was like, "Really? A .38 Special in the side of the door? On our way to the gayest, friendliest city ever?"

At first, our sex life was kind of the same. And then it just stopped. Like he didn't even want to have sex with me. I think he was under so much emotional stress that he just didn't have a sex drive—which is understandable. But he's this macho guy from Montana, it's not like he's gonna say, "I feel like my emotions are running so out of control that I don't have a sex drive." That's not a conversation he knew how to have. He wouldn't go to therapy, and he refused to acknowledge that he was having any issues. So things just kept getting worse and worse.

One time, we had a Saturday off together, so I was like, "Let's go on a picnic in the National Park." I love doing little romantic things like that. We were supposed to go at two o'clock, and I came into the kitchen at one o'clock to start making the food and he was eating. And I'm like, "I thought we were going on a picnic." And he was like, "I fucking work and I fucking make money and I fill this fridge with food and I'll eat when I want. What, you're gonna tell me when I can eat now?"

And I was just like, "What? *No.* I thought we were going on a picnic. What is your problem?"

Then he would turn it into this whole "What the fuck is *your* problem? I'm just eating! I'm just eating some lunch!" He had all this pent-up rage—it's almost like he would *want* to argue. He would yell right in my face and I was just like, "What are you doing? People don't just yell in people's faces!"

Another night, we were back home in Montana, and we were at this bar near his mom's house. It's kinda trashy, but it's fun. So this kid comes in—it's his twenty-first birthday—and he's with all his friends, they're these big Indian guys. And Billy somehow winds up outside with this birthday kid. They start throwing around a little and then one of his friends, this big fucking Indian guy, starts punching Billy in the face—*hard*.

He throws him into my car; my side-view mirror goes flying off. Billy's just pouring blood. And he's like, "Who hit me?" And the Indian guy was about to be all, "Bitch, *I* hit you!" But I was like, "It was the kid! The kid hit you! It was a lucky punch— *let's go*." Because the last thing I need is my husband going up to the Indian guy, "Oh, you hit me?" I mean, this guy would have killed him. And they *will* kill you. They're Native American, the law has no jurisdiction on their reservation. If you disappear on the res—you're *gone*.

The next day his face is all swollen and he's like, "That kid did not hit me." And I'm like, "You're right, the big Indian guy hit you. But it was time to go. Like, what were you thinking? What if you punched that guy and they were like, 'Fuck you, little white boy, we're taking your girlfriend'? You put me in danger, dude!" Then he was all angry with me because I lied to him. It was always crazy stuff like that where I was like, "What are we even fighting about? We're a married couple, why are we getting in bar fights? *What is going on?*"

I would talk to the other military wives about it. One of them, her husband . . . it's so crazy. The Afghanis, they all wear these prayer bracelets. So after he killed them, he'd take them home to his wife, "I got you these bracelets." And she was like, "You got me bracelets off of people you killed? What the hell is going on in your head? I don't want these in my house!" She told me, "My husband has punched so many holes in the wall that I feel like I go to Home Depot every week to buy a new can of spackle."

Everything came to a head for us at the big Marine Corps Ball in Vegas. That's where all the guys put on their dress blues and you put on a ball gown and it's this big, fancy thing. We were trying to make it a really good time for us, it was gonna be this fresh start.

When we got there, the hotel was like, "You have to put down a two-hundred-dollar holding deposit." So we ended up with less money to play with—and Billy got pissed. It's like, "Dude, all you have to do is play nickel slots and you can drink for free. There's buffets everywhere. Whatever, we're young, let's just have fun." But he was like, "We're not managing our money well!" And I'm like, "If it's a big deal, I can just call my parents, they can wire us five hundred dollars—it's not a big deal." And that pissed him off even more.

So he leaves, says he's going to have a beer. He doesn't come back until 2:00 A.M. At that point I was like, "I'm done, give me the keys, I'm leaving. I don't want to go to the stupid Marine Ball."

And he starts yelling in my face, just being really crazy, "Fuck you! I've got the keys!" He shuts the hotel room door. "You're not going anywhere!"

Now I'm like, "I will call the police."

He *rips* the hotel phone out of the wall, *throws* it across the room. Throws my cell phone across the room. Like, "Bitch, you're not calling anybody!" Just *psycho*. He had been a little violent with me before, like pushed me down and that kind of thing. So I'm like, "Fuck you, I will start screaming!" And he, um . . .

He just choked me until I lost consciousness.

I woke up and I was like, "What just happened? Did I just have a seizure?" And I looked at him, he was standing over me, and he just went stone cold. No emotion. Nothing. He just walked over and sat in the chair.

And I was just like, "You just choked the shit out of me and almost killed me and now you're sitting there as calm as day? *Oh, my God.*" I'm really scared now, thinking I'm gonna be found between some mattresses in Vegas. Like, this is not how I want to go out, y'know?

He calls his buddy Steve: "Sharon and I are in a fight, you wanna get a drink or something?" Just fucking calm as can be.

So Steve and his wife come up and they're all drunk and having a blast, like, "Hey!"

And I was like, "He just choked me. *He just fucking choked me.*"

And they're like, "What?"

And Billy's like, "What are you talking about? What are you saying?"

And I was like, "Are you kidding? You just fucking attacked me!"

I started bawling. I looked insane and he looked completely calm, when in reality it was so the opposite. He's like, "You're just pissed that I was out having a good time all night and you're in the room. I can't believe you would say this to my friends. What are you trying to do?" And I was just like, "Oh, fuck, you are beyond crazy." It's one thing to freak out but then to be emotionless and pretend that I was making it up? This is a whole other level.

How do you know when it's time to leave? When it gets violent. I mean, if it happens once, okay, get some therapy, get some help. But if it happens more than once, get out. *Go.* There's no place for violence in a marriage. In *any* relationship.

For me, when my husband choked me, that's not when I realized. I mean, it was definitely a huge eye-opener, like, I probably shouldn't be in this marriage, but it wasn't *the moment*. It was later, when we got into another argument, and he said something like, "You're such a fucking bitch all the time. See, that's why you got choked."

And I was like, "Oh, *hell,* no!" That's when I was like, "You are not sorry. In your mind, you completely justified what you did."

I did have a lot of guilt when I decided to leave him because I do believe that when you marry someone you've made that commitment, and I'm fiercely loyal about things like that. But I honestly felt like I had no choice, like he was going to end up seriously hurting me. Literally everyone in my life was like,

"Sharon, you're depressed, you hate yourself, you're unhappy. You've already had more than one violent experience. What are you waiting for? Do you need to end up in a wheelchair? Do you need to die?"

Looking back, yeah, I think that there's a little more I could have done. When his anger/rage things got worse, I should have reported that. I should have gone to his command and said, "Look, he's not okay, this is what's happening." Because if I'd done that, he would have been forced to have mandatory therapy. But I didn't. I was like, "Oh, he just got back from a war, and if I say something then it's going to hurt him. He's a very good marine. He worked very hard, he's been promoted with honors several times, and if this comes out, there's going to be this mark on his record." So I didn't want to do that. But looking back, had I done that, it might have saved our marriage.

Right now I'm kind of at this weird crossroads in my dating life where I want someone to have wine and cheese with, read poetry, share recipes, and have kids with. But at the same time, I want to be with someone who's a *guy*. Like if we had to survive, he could snap a bunny's neck and feed me, y'know?

How do you really get to know someone? Travel together. Because something always goes wrong when you're traveling. You're gonna eat something bad, you're gonna have to shit, you're gonna be in a hotel room, and it's gonna be so ugly. Because when girls date, we're *fabulous*. We spend an hour getting ready. We dress up, we wear our makeup and our high heels. But when I go home and I'm having an evening by myself, I put on a face mask, get in my sweatpants, eat some Indian food, watch *Bones*. Would I do that in front of a guy I wanted to date? *Never.* You don't want to do that right off the bat, like, "Bam! Here's my sweatpants. *What's up?* Wanna eat Indian food?" Um, no.

That's why it's a good idea to have some uncomfortable experiences together. Do something that requires you to not be in makeup for an entire weekend. Go camping. It might rain and you might get grumpy. Or if you're traveling, you might miss your connecting flight and then you're stuck in the airport. Or you're on a plane and there's a baby next to you screaming the entire time. How's that guy gonna handle it? Is he gonna be like, "Shut that fucking baby up!"? If so, there you go. That's not the guy you want to marry. But if he's making cute faces and trying to cheer the baby up? That's a step in the right direction.

"The fact that divorce is a possibility is probably a good thing for making people stay on their toes. If you knew for a fact that this person was going to be yours till the day you die, you might really become complacent and make no effort."

ALIAS: Paul

OCCUPATION: Chef

YEAR OF BIRTH: 1977

CURRENT MARRIAGE STATUS: Divorced

DO YOU HAVE ANY CHILDREN? No

WHERE YOU GREW UP: Europe

WHERE YOU LIVE: Oregon

YEAR OF MARRIAGE: 2004

HOW LONG YOU DATED BEFORE YOU WERE MARRIED: Six
    months

YEAR OF DIVORCE: 2011

You met your wife in 2004, the year that Facebook launched. Was it old-fashioned love at first sight?
Actually, when I first saw her I was like, *She's out of my league— I'm not even going to bother talking to her.* She was just so beautiful. And then my standoffishness kind of worked in my favor.

She misinterpreted your insecurity as coolness?
Yeah, exactly.

How old were you guys?
She was nineteen, I was twenty-seven—but I was twenty-seven going on nineteen, and she was nineteen going on twenty-seven. We got married after six months but it was almost like we were waiting as long as possible. We probably would have gotten married after three weeks, it was just so wonderful and intense.

Do you remember any stories about how you clicked right at the beginning?

No, it wasn't like that. It was more about this space that opened up between us when we were together. I think when you're really, deeply in love with someone there's this feeling that you've created something together, which is this love, and it starts to permeate every aspect of your existence. In the early days it expresses itself most strongly through sexual passion. You just can't get enough of each other and you're waking up in the middle of the night and having sex. You feel so alive, discovering another person and discovering yourself. And then, of course, that evolves and gives way to a different type of complicity.

How do you nurture and sustain that kind of partner-in-crime connection?

I decided early on that I wasn't going to mess this up. I'm not going to be unfaithful, I'm not going to do anything to jeopardize the sanctity of this. That's the beautiful thing about marriage—in its best form it's like a little island of the sacred, and the culture doesn't have much of that. I said "sacred," so I should define that. It places it above your everyday whims. There's a tendency to prioritize our desires as being the most important thing, but they're not. When you get married, you're saying: "I'm making this commitment—this is something more important than the way I feel today." And that type of commitment can give meaning to a life.

Is there a shadow side as well?

Well, there's also a very cynical definition of love, I can't remember who said it. "Love is nothing but the sexual attraction of the young, the habituation of the middle-aged, and the mutual dependence of the old." And there's some truth to that, too.

One of the men I interviewed said that the key to a good marriage is finding someone who accepts you for who you

**are and then tells you that that's not good enough. And with
their help, you figure out how to get better. And you have to
do the same thing for them. Do you think that's true?**
Yeah, that's true. But it's a very fine line. One can become *too*
critical of one's partner. Or too acquiescent. I just think that the
essential ingredient for a successful relationship is really allowing the other person to be themselves. It's very easy for men
or women to find someone who they can dominate, someone
who's going to do exactly what they want and not challenge them
in any way. So that is key: finding somebody who is really wor-
thy of you.

Would you prefer a critic or a fan?
I prefer a fan who is also honest and who helps push you, like
you said. It would be a general kind of support mixed with constructive criticism.

**Do you require your spouse to be a muse at some level, a col-
laborator?**
I do require that, yeah.

**I've been reading this book about married sex called *Mat-
ing in Captivity,* and the author says that most people want
safety and consistency in their day-to-day lives, but that
those qualities can make for a boring sex life. Do you think
it's a good idea to foster elements of mystery, risk, and taboo
in the bedroom?**
I think we can see those roles more as games, which is what they
are, but we should still play them well. "Playing games" has this
horrible connotation, but "playing" has a great connotation, and
games are supposed to be fun. You can be a very caring man in
the sense of having a lot of traditional feminine qualities—being
more nurturing than dominant, for example—but you can still
play the dominant game in bed. It's like what you were talking

about—you don't want to lose that mystery altogether. You have to find ways of keeping it alive.

What do you think about these tips for keeping it alive: limit nonsexual nudity, no laptops in bed, don't go to the bathroom with the door open, no pictures of each other's parents by the bed?
I think all those things are great ideas. Those subtle desexualizers, all those cliché things that make you see the person as less attractive.

Is there a danger in feeling too safe, too secure in a relationship?
The fact that divorce is a possibility is probably a good thing for making people stay on their toes. If you knew for a fact that this person was going to be yours till the day you die, you might really become complacent and make no effort. Not only for the other person, but for yourself, too.

Did you ever cheat on your wife?
I never did, amazingly. And it felt really good because I've been unfaithful in every other relationship. Either actually cheating or being in an open thing, so this was my only stab at true, monogamous fidelity. And there's something to be said for it. Again, it goes back to that sanctity. We're only going to have this between us.

Did she ever cheat on you?
I don't think so.

Your ex-wife is famous and beautiful. Did you ever feel not so attractive by comparison?
I was lucky to be married to one of the most beautiful women in the world, but you know the Jack Nicholson line, right? "Show

me the most beautiful woman in the world and I'll show you a man who's tired of fucking her." But that's cyclical. Sometimes they look better, sometimes they look worse. Sometimes you're like, "You look great today!" And sometimes you're like, "Why are you wearing that?" You have to cultivate the desire to want to impress the other person and keep up your appearance.

You were married for seven years. When did things start to deteriorate?
I don't think "deteriorate" is the right word. We went from being lovers to being great friends. It was a very gradual change. I don't want to say that that was the only problem; there were other, more subtle shifts in the power dynamic. She was making a lot more money and living in this limelight.

Was it emasculating to have a wife that was more powerful?
I don't know. . . . She was ten times more successful and powerful than me and it's tricky because I'm very open-minded and I consider myself to be a feminist and I was actually very proud and excited by the fact that she was doing so well. But there are these deep-seated cultural things and no matter how much you question them on the surface, there's a sense that the man has to be the breadwinner. And in many ways, she had taken the role of the husband in the relationship. Going off and working and I was keeping the house nice. And I embraced that role.

And the elasticity of that space was good—separating and coming back together?
That's what was so great about our relationship and why it survived—*thrived,* even. Because we would miss each other. She'd come home and I'd be excited to hear what happened and she'd be excited to hear what I was doing. And you have to preserve that. If you're together all the time and you become this little unit, it's threatening to you being an entire human being.

That's been coming up a lot in these interviews—the difference between fusing and losing your identity.

In this day and age, it's a recipe for disaster if you try and control the other person. To a certain degree, you have to be autonomous. You can't make the person feel like if they weren't there then you would be nothing or that you would be destroyed. You really should be coming together to support each other, to depend on each other, to love each other—but not to possess.

Right, and of course there's a big difference between depending on each other and becoming codependent.

That's why honesty is important. You have to establish realistic boundaries and at least acknowledge that the other person needs to live a life that's not all about you. And just know that you'll benefit from that because you're going to have a more complete human being that's coming home to you.

Who suggested that you split up?

Oh, it was her. It was definitely her.

What did she say?

She came back from a job and I could just tell that she wasn't in it anymore. So then there was this terrible anxiety for months, wondering if I could do something to save it. That was the worst experience of my life. Like three months of not sleeping.

What did you suggest doing to save it?

I wanted to go to therapy. She wasn't into it. I wanted to try something less drastic than divorce. Separate for a year, see how that goes. But I think she'd gotten it in her head that it was over and I couldn't blame her because that same desire to jump into something full force is the reason we got married to begin with.

Were you getting on each other's nerves, fighting a lot?
In some relationships it's probably much more dramatic, the way it turns sour, but we didn't have that. It was much more subtle, our growing apart. The relationship was becoming much more platonic. The balance of power shifted in a way that was no longer making me feel like I was the best version of me. Maybe there was a certain amount of emasculation.

Did you feel rejected by her?
Yeah, I guess I would say I started to feel a little rejected toward the end. I mean, we had such an incredible sex life for years and years. But there's that great saying: "The distance to love is like wind to a flame. It puts out the small ones and makes the big ones even bigger."

Did you suggest trying an open relationship?
I did suggest an open marriage, yeah. I think that would be an interesting thing to explore. But not *completely* open because no matter how open-minded you are, you're going to have a certain amount of possessiveness and insecurity that your mate was with somebody else.

So how do you find the right balance?
That's a big question. Let's say you're going to stay married for thirty years—should there be a safety valve? Not like you're going to indiscriminately go out and fuck anybody else—not to be exploitive, not to be disrespectful. But it's kind of tacitly approved that the marriage is about more than sex. You're going to have children, you want to know that this person is going to be there for the rest of your life. But the sexual element, it's not possible to sustain that for fifty years.

Why do you think that?
I met a woman who's eighty-seven and she's married to a ninety-

181

three-year-old man—they've been together for like sixty years—
and she said, "You know about realpolitik? Well, there's a thing
called real relationship. Let me put it another way: We don't ask
too many questions of each other." And I wonder about these
marriages that last that long, if that's necessary.

**I think that's the most delicate balance—between commit-
ment and freedom.**
Have you read *Against Love* by Laura Kipnis? She says that in
older cultures marriage was very unequal in the sense that the
woman became the property of a man and she would be at home
and be domestic and he could go off and frolic and be with other
women. And she says that what's happened is that rather than
bringing the woman up to the man's level, we brought the man
down to the woman's level. And now we're *both* these enslaved
creatures in a marriage.

Enslaved by our idealism?
She says that everything we look at is propagandizing for the
idea that this is what we should want. Every movie, every bill-
board, every image that we see, it's a form of social control that
has taken the place of repressive government or repressive work
conditions. And so now you have the couple—these institu-
tions—that are set up to control our behavior.

**You grew up abroad. What did you learn from your Euro-
pean background in terms of what to do and what not to do
in a marriage?**
We learned a lot. Simple things like: Don't sit together when
you go out to dinner with other people. In America, if you have
a table of ten people, they seat the couples together, which is a
terrible idea because (a) you have nothing to talk about when you
get home because you've been with each other the whole time.

And (b) there's nothing more boring than sitting next to a couple that has this kind of insular feeling.

Do you think that Europeans have a less idealistic view of marriage and fidelity?

In older cultures, I do think there is less of an idealism. Here, people are married for thirty years and then you find out one person was unfaithful and then they leave each other. And I think that's crazy. I don't think marriages—or any relationship—should end over action. It should end over a broader growing apart or a realization that things aren't working. Often, the action is used as an excuse because they don't want to talk about the bigger things, so then they say, "Okay, now I have a good reason." People shouldn't have that as an ethos—it's not about "you did this" or "I did that." It's about: "Who have we become as human beings and are we going to continue doing this together?"

Would she say that you were always supportive of her?

In the end, I think I was *too* supportive. I was a little bit too eager to please. One of the reasons why I've been so successful in long relationships is because I avoid confrontation to a fault.

You seem very communicative.

I'm communicative but I'm extremely diplomatic. I don't see being right as that important. I can know for myself that I'm right, I don't need to convince the other person.

Do you have any tips about how to fight fairly and productively with your wife?

Yes, it's important not to be too high-and-mighty. Take responsibility for your own feelings. *Own* your feelings. There's a tendency in couples to try to lay your problems on the other person but that's not a good idea at all.

Could you have been a better husband?

No, I think I was a very good husband. I remember, she said these key words that I'll always think about. She said, "You're the perfect husband—I wouldn't change a thing about you. Unfortunately, I don't want a husband right now." And how can you argue with that?

Right, I've learned that when one person wants out, it's done. Okay, last question, getting back to what we were talking about earlier. How can we resist the propaganda and dial back our idealism in the service of *true* true love—not the fairy-tale version?

We have to not overly prioritize the eternal. This is a basic tenet of existentialist philosophy. The finitude of existence is what gives it significance. And the relationship is a key way that you see that. There is always the danger and the possibility and the probability that it's going to end. But instead of using that as a rationale for a cynical outlook you should see that as an opportunity to lend poignancy to the moments you have.

How?

There are two ways marriage can end: either divorce or death. Both horrible, right? So you can either dwell on that or you can say, "We're living a finite thing, let's really appreciate every moment, let's have gratitude for it."

"Sometimes people mistake brutality for honesty, and there is no need to stomp on anyone's feelings in the name of being honest."

ALIAS: Mary

OCCUPATION: Librarian

DATE OF BIRTH: 1957

CURRENT MARRIAGE STATUS: Divorced

DO YOU HAVE ANY CHILDREN? Two. Twenty-three and twenty-one

WHERE YOU GREW UP: Ohio

WHERE YOU LIVE: New Hampshire

YEAR OF MARRIAGE: 1986

HOW LONG YOU DATED BEFORE YOU WERE MARRIED: Ten months

YEAR OF DIVORCE: 2000

The biggest mistake people make when they get married is to expect that their spouse will somehow make them whole. *Wrong.* You have to be whole *already* in order to share a part of yourself with someone else. If you're not, the relationship is going to suck the life out of the other person. All this "joined together" and the "two become one" stuff is just a bunch of unhealthy, emotional crap. Two people can live together and be committed to each other without fusing their identities. With atoms it makes a big explosion, y'know?

There's a book called *It's Never About What It's About* and I would have to agree with that. The little things seem to get under one's skin, but for the most part I believe that we use those things as tools to clobber our partners about something else entirely, some bigger issue. Like picking a scab. The underlying wound can't heal if all we do is pick at the scab on top.

I don't think you have to agree on silly things like who likes white meat and who likes dark meat, or who wants the thermostat set to seventy-five and who wants it set to sixty-five. Temperament is important; temperature is not. But I'll be damned if

185

the things that attract people to each other in the first place don't become the very things that drive you nuts. What starts out as "free-spirited" can end up as "irresponsible." The person who was so "steady" and "reliable" can wind up looking like an awful old fart.

One of the main things that attracted me to my ex, who is a pastor, was that he was so attentive to the members of his congregation. I admired his tremendous work ethic. I thought, "What a great dad he'll be." But after a while I resented him because his work always came first and the kids and I were somewhere south of tenth place. He was never, ever, in fourteen years of marriage, late for a church service or meeting. But do you think he could get home in time for dinner? Not a chance.

Honesty, like passion, is overrated. You need to reveal the secrets that could come back and bite you on the rear end. Ask yourself, "Will my partner flip out when he finds out about this?" If the answer is "yes"—or even "maybe"—you'd better fess up in advance. But I don't think that you are under any obligation to discuss your prior love/sex life (unless you have a communicable disease). And you don't have to say absolutely everything that pops into your head. Sometimes people mistake brutality for honesty, and there is no need to stomp on anyone's feelings in the name of being honest.

The biggest lie I told my ex was that I loved him. I was never sexually attracted to him, nor he to me, probably. I married because I wanted to have a family. *Any dick in a storm,* if you will. He was the sperm donor and I was the baby carriage. I don't think he told me any biggies, either—except perhaps about loving me, too. But there was one whopper of an omission.

I was pregnant with our second child and it was our fourth wedding anniversary. I happened to be in his office at the church when he took a call from the conference minister. His face went white as a sheet, and when he hung up the phone, I asked him what she said. He answered, "I have to go to a meeting right now." I knew he was lying through his teeth, and I told him to tell me the truth, which he did.

He said that twenty or so years ago, when he was a pastor in his first church, one of the boys from the youth group spent the night at his house and they slept together. And now the young man was in counseling and revealed that information to his counselor, who apparently reported it to the conference minister, who got right on the phone with my husband to try to figure out some damage control. And there was even more to the story. At one of his later parishes, he was arrested for soliciting sex from a male undercover police officer, but the charges were later dropped. He said it was all a misunderstanding, but that was bullshit.

So there I am, seven months pregnant, and I just find out that my husband is probably gay at the very least and a pervert at worst. He had to go to a support group for sex offenders for quite a while after that, and how it never got out to his congregation (or future congregations), I will never know. I never breathed a word of it for ten years, but finally it was killing me and I told my sister and a few friends. No one ever ratted him out to the best of my knowledge. My children have asked me many times if their dad is gay, but I don't say anything.

If you ask a man who his best friend is, he'll likely name his wife. If you ask a woman, she'll name another woman. I think that men have more to lose when a marriage goes sour. My dad always said that good marriages rely on "mutual interdependence." He brought home most of the bacon, and my mother did everything else—bought his clothes, laid them out in the morning, drove him to work, picked him up, made his lunch every day. One time I figured out that she'd probably made over seven thousand grilled cheese sandwiches in her lifetime. I can remember her walking by him and he'd reach out and pat her on the fanny and say, "I love you, baby."

Have I ever been in love? No. I've had relationships, but they have all been unhealthy in some way or another. I do believe that I have *been* loved. In fact, in all but one of my relationships I've been the one to pull the plug. Am I jaded? Uh, what do you think? Yeah, I'm pretty jaded. In the best of relationships there is an element of "putting up with" and I don't think I'm willing to put up with anything anymore. I have reached my crap quota for this lifetime. I love my dog and he loves me. It works. Would I ever get married again? I say no, but who knows? Someday I might actually fall in love and then it will all be up for grabs.

I do have some wonderful male friends, including the first man I ever had sex with. He's like my brother now. If I had married him I think we could have been happy together. His marriage failed, too, and he did not remarry. Sometimes I think it would be fun to be roomies when our kids are grown and gone, but I think sexual tension might ruin it—for me, anyway.

Maybe when he's older and impotent from blood pressure medication. Oh, wait. There's that damn Viagra shit. You know, that has really ruined the lives of middle-aged women around the world who want nothing more than to get a good night's sleep.

"I just wish I'd taken the time to let us get bored with each other and then to see if we really had what it takes to recultivate the romance."

ALIAS: Nicole

OCCUPATION: Graduate student

YEAR OF BIRTH: 1981

CURRENT MARRIAGE STATUS: Divorced

DO YOU HAVE ANY CHILDREN? No

WHERE YOU GREW UP: Rhode Island

WHERE YOU LIVE: Massachusetts

YEAR OF MARRIAGE: 2008

HOW LONG YOU DATED BEFORE YOU WERE MARRIED: A year and
    a half

YEAR OF DIVORCE: 2010

I thought Alan was hot. I liked his Robert Smith hair and hipster clothes. He was intelligent, clever, and deeply kind. He had all these creative pursuits that he was really engaged in and pretty good at but he didn't seem to have any illusions about being able to make a living doing them. We seemed to have compatible beliefs, priorities, and aspirations—we weren't going to be khaki pants–wearing suburban homeowners with stable forty-hour-a-week jobs. He also has this absolutely infectious enthusiasm that can make the world seem like an almost magical place, and when we started dating, he got really enthusiastic about me. I felt calmed, like he smoothed out my rough edges, in a good way. I didn't feel like I was losing myself at all, I almost felt like I was free and whole for the first time. I got completely swept up in romantic ideals, in the absolutely dizzying effects of the most intense infatuation I'd ever experienced.

But some of those things began to change even before we got married. He gained some weight and stopped paying as much attention to how he looked, and his creative output slowed dramatically. Instead, he began spending most of his time playing video games and watching television, drinking to excess, and eating delivery pizza and chicken fingers. The shiny, new relationship enthusiasm wore off so he stopped making me feel special and incredible. But the biggest changes were probably with me. I began to realize that a shared rejection of conventional aspirations doesn't necessarily mean you have *compatible* aspirations. I just wish I'd taken the time to let us get bored with each other and then to see if we really had what it takes to recultivate the romance and to change with each other.

By the time we got married, it was like there was no reason to try to impress, entertain, or charm anymore. We slept at completely different times and almost never in our bed. Due to some finds on Craigslist, we had three couches and we slept separately so regularly that we'd refer to them as our "his and hers couches." We also had such different food habits and tastes. When we went grocery shopping, we'd each get our own things and pay separately, like roommates. Not *even* roommates—I've shared food expenses and meals with some of my roommates!

I felt lonely, but couldn't identify it as loneliness. How could I be lonely married to the love of my life? We had settled into a routine where we only had sex once a week or so, maybe even less. There was no variety, no real mental or emotional rewards—just physical pleasure. There was none of the urgency or tension that makes sex so great—that sense of wanting to *impress* or *entice* someone. I also got really precious about conditions being just right. I had this idea that if I had sex when I didn't really want to, I would start to associate it with being a chore or a burden and start to hate it. So I turned down or discouraged advances if I wasn't already "in the mood," which in turn made him less likely to make advances. Plus, he had really bad breath, which never bothered me when we were dating, but gradually it made it so that I never wanted to kiss him and I resented his lack of oral hygiene.

Eventually, it started to seem like he didn't have any aspirations at all. And instead of feeling like we were going to have this great, adventurous, rich, full life together, I started to feel like I didn't have anything to look forward to with him. Neither of us felt appreciated, not in the most critical ways. I can be cold and rigid, disdainful. I don't like that about myself. I see it in my dad, a cruel indifference to my mother's feelings, and I was doing it to Alan. Making him feel stupid, thinking he was being lazy and weak and losing respect for him as he wallowed in video games and indecision.

We talked about everything a lot, tried to think of things we could do, but rarely came up with concrete changes so we never really fixed anything. It was a big issue in the fight we had the night before I went to Canada with a group of old friends, and I wound up cheating on Alan with my ex, Dan.

From my journal:

Both Alan and I kept telling ourselves independently and collectively that we were happy. Lucky to be so happy. Lucky to be married to people we considered our equals. Happy. Happy. Happy. It became a kind of mantra: "I'm happy, with you and with us."

At least once a week we'd go out, or stay in, and get drunk together and have great conversation, like always. But we have both been lonely. The night before I went to Canada, Alan and I barely slept while we complained about how disconnected we felt. As always, we failed to make plans to change, defended our habits, and finally, exhausted, offered reaffirmations of love.

"I'm really happy, with you, with us."

And so, then, Canada.

The five of us (Abby, Jill, Ari, Dan, me) drink five bottles of wine the first night, there is Scrabble and Rumble Racing. And one by one Abby and Jill and Ari go to bed. But Dan and I are still awake because I do not ever want this to end, and I don't remember now how it came up, but

191

suddenly we are talking about how it's still difficult sometimes for him to see me. And there are feelings that I assumed I'd more or less buried, but now they are all rushing back and I don't know what to do, and it is late, late when on the porch after chain smoking and so much crying, he kisses me. And I kiss him back and then stop him—shove him away. And he wilts and then I hug him and what did I just do?

Back inside to pour some whiskey, eventually outside and splashing in the water. The two of us go upstairs and sleep together in the bottom bunk of the first room at the top of the stairs. The rest of the weekend is a blur of cooking, falling asleep with books on various couches, video games, and affection I should turn down, but it feels honest and inevitable and necessary.

How can I possibly defend this? It is indefensible. Selfish, impulsive, and devastating.

We slept in the same bed the next night, and the next. I had sex with him. The sex was rushed and weirdly dispassionate, not even that good. I think it is worse that I am in love with him but I'm horrified by how powerless I felt to stop something knowing how much it would hurt Alan.

I am a compulsive child and should not be trusted with love.

I met Dan shortly before I moved to Massachusetts in 2004. He was dating someone casually but we met up when I visited Cambridge to find a place to live and we ended up making out in my rental car at the end of the night. He broke up with the other girl and we started dating when I moved to town.

Lots of possible reasons why it didn't work. I thought he was really great, which made me kind of nervous around him. Instead of wearing off over time, it just seemed to get worse. The first few times we hung out, conversation flowed really naturally and we seemed to have great chemistry. But once we were actually dating, that just evaporated. He just wasn't emotionally available. I was the one who broke it off after three or four months because it was obvious he wasn't that into me.

Afterward, we started trying to do the whole "let's just be

friends" thing. I wasn't desperately seeking affirmation that wasn't there anymore and all the awkwardness of dating was just gone. So we became really good friends. We went out for beers at least once a week, drove to New York to see shows every other month or so, went to cafés to play chess or Scrabble, chatted online all the time. We traveled together—the first annual trip to Canada with Abby and Jill and Ari was in 2006. When I went to New York to find a wedding dress, Dan came along. He actually helped me pick out the dress.

At our wedding, I asked him to give a toast. It was great, really touching, it made lots of people cry. That night, Alan went to bed around 1:00 A.M. or so. We got married at a B&B and we were staying in one of the rooms there. Most of the guests were staying at a hotel a couple blocks away. Alan's best friend since childhood had a really early flight the next morning and was talking about trying to just stay up. So Abby, Dan, and I decided to stay up with him.

On the way back to their hotel, I was walking with Dan and thanking him for the toast, and just generally feeling an overwhelming amount of love. I took his hand as we were walking—and that felt really intimate but totally "right." At the time I thought of it as the perfect ending to the perfect day. I even mentioned it in the journal entry I wrote about our wedding.

Later, Alan said something about that hurting him. He was angry that I had gone back to their hotel rather than coming up to our room, but I figured he'd just be passed out anyway. In retrospect, this seems obvious and I'm a fool for thinking the hand-holding was just a normal, friendly, affectionate gesture.

My parents' marriage seemed so miserable that for most of my life I thought I would never get married. I imagine they must have had a loving relationship at some point, but for as long as I can remember, my mom has done all the domestic labor, unhappily, and my father treats her like an idiot. When I was very young, I remember them fighting a lot. When he'd be mean to her, she would always stand up for herself. Then one night when I was about seven, they'd been fighting and she came into my room, crying. She asked me if I wanted to go for a drive. We just drove around the suburbs for what felt like hours while tears streamed down her face. And it seemed like she stopped fighting back after that.

Years later, when I was home from college, they got into an argument about something trivial, like the best way to get somewhere, and my dad was just unrelenting. My mom left the room in tears. The next day, she asked me if I had said something to him, because apparently he had apologized. I guess maybe my presence made him more self-conscious. But what really struck me was that not only is he an asshole to her all the time, but his apologizing was so out of character that she thought I must have put him up to it.

I wouldn't have gotten married if I thought I was going to get divorced. I do consider it a failure of self-knowledge, of prudence and temperance, of humility and foresight. I think I was really hasty and arrogant and thoughtless. I was so sure I had loved Alan, so sure we would work together to get through things—that enough love, trust, and willingness could make any marriage work.

It should have been a long relationship with a shitty breakup. Instead, I promised someone I would love them and do anything in my power to foster our relationship, and then cheated on him and left him for someone else. I hurt someone I loved so badly and I can never take that back. And I let down not only him but also my family and his family and everyone who came to our wedding and believed in me. It's probably the worst mistake I've ever made.

I don't know if I'm really wiser because of it but I think I'm less arrogant and maybe that's a kind of wisdom. A friend told me recently that she's trying to hold happiness lightly without grasping it. I think through the humbling, painful process of divorce, I learned to do that a little better. I'm also a lot happier, assisted in no small way by my relationship with Dan, which has flourished. We're getting married this summer.

"Have the argument and dissolve it before you decide to take the nuclear option of having an affair."

ALIAS: Adam

OCCUPATION: Sales

YEAR OF BIRTH: 1977

CURRENT MARRIAGE STATUS: Divorced

DO YOU HAVE ANY CHILDREN? Yes. Two boys—six and four

WHERE YOU GREW UP: West Virginia

WHERE YOU LIVE: New York

YEAR OF MARRIAGE: 2006

HOW LONG YOU DATED BEFORE YOU WERE MARRIED: Six years

YEAR OF DIVORCE: 2012

I was married to a woman for six years—I still am for another month or so—but the marriage was over at least two years ago. My wife left me for another man. They started dating. Can you really call it dating, or was it simply fucking? I'm not yet sure. I guess for now we can call it dating, since she now lives with him. With my two children.

My first son was born in 2006 and shortly thereafter my wife and I decided to move closer to her parents. I use that term "we" loosely here. "We" decided to move away from our friends, our careers, and our charming first home, to be closer to her family. Interestingly, we never discussed moving closer to my family. That should have been a red flag, because while I got along great with her family, I had no idea she harbored such bad feelings toward mine.

So we moved, without securing jobs, and it was unbeknownst to me that her plan was to stay home and raise our children. I would go to work in this strange, new place, where I knew no one, and she would live a life of leisure—a life that her mother raised her to believe she was entitled to. See, my wife believes in the fairy tales you see in mushy, romantic comedies starring Kate Hudson or Hugh Grant. In fact, in the midst of my paranoia about her affair, we discussed this. I remember saying, "That's why it's a movie, it's an escape from reality, an ideal." And her response was, "Well, why *can't* it be like that?"

I knew then that she was cheating on me but she made me feel like I was paranoid and crazy to think it. I said to both her and her dipshit boyfriend—well, he was just a "friend" at the time—that if they were doing what I thought they were doing, it was the most brazen move I'd ever seen. But asking a cheater if they're cheating turned out to be a futile effort—go figure.

So I spied.

My wife's "fairy tale" included more time at the gym than ever. Yes, I know, how *dare* I question her time at the gym, I must not have wanted her to be healthy or to better herself, right? No, I just wanted her to be home in time for dinner with our boys like she told them she would. You see, Mr. Wonderful is a has-been bodybuilder who works with my wife. Her "fairy tale" also included electrolysis of everything south of her belly button. There were appointments to be kept, there was even a gift certificate purchased by her mom as a Christmas present for the express purpose of beautifying her nether regions. Yes, that's the very same mom who "loved" me as a son in-law.

Her "fairy tale" also included multiple purchases from Victoria's Secret—well, at least so far as my credit cards were concerned, and judging by the daily spam sent to her e-mail in-box. Yes, I saw her e-mail because I was able to get her passwords through key logging software I added to the computer. I couldn't find anything on her cell phone—she must have had him on auto-delete or something—but I intercepted an e-mail with sixty-some-odd bullet points as to why Mr. Wonderful would like to grow old with my wife. Yes, bullet points. And though I'd like to call attention to his lack of creativity in writing a lengthy e-mail in bullet-point format, it's clear from the content that he is in fact *very* creative. Kudos to him; I had no idea that my wife liked to do all that stuff. Apparently there was good reason for the electrolysis.

I think it's important to know that I never felt worse about myself than when I started spying. I felt so awful to betray her trust, because I wanted so badly to believe that she was telling me the truth. But the affair was already too damaging to our marriage. She trusted, confided in, spent time with—everything you're supposed to do with your spouse, she did with another man. And she did it overtly, by choice, and she cast aside time with her children and me to do it. That, to me, is far worse than the actual sex acts, though those were vomit-inducing to read. I did in fact vomit when I read that e-mail for the first time. I had been lied to just a couple hours earlier, and then to read it in detail was more than I could handle.

One of my friends told me throughout all of this that I had to "have the argument" with her. I suppose he meant "discussion," but he always used the word "argument." My wife let her dissatisfaction fester and said nothing until she found someone else to talk to. That is the advice I would give anyone getting married. Have the argument and dissolve it before you decide to take the nuclear option of having an affair. That's selfish and cowardly. Because if it was worth getting married in the first place, it's worth an argument to clarify things. Otherwise you're not being honest with yourself—you're hiding. And you can't be together if you're hiding.

The crazy part is, if asked to do it all again, I'd get married. I'd even marry *her* again—so long as it was the woman I married, and not the person I'm divorcing. I remember thinking to myself when we met in college, "Wow, she's so grown up, so put together." I saw in her what I lacked in myself. I have at times thought myself to be "put together," but it's clear to me now that those were fleeting moments and that I've mostly floated through life with some level of charm. In many ways, in my marriage, I guess that charm wore off.

These are the thoughts I have from time to time when I'm feeling particularly saddened by it all, when I feel as though my contribution to the end of my marriage is more me than her. But then I remember—she married me for me. I've always been the same person, albeit with more or less confidence and bravado, depending on how things are going. So then I get angry thinking about the times we spent together, twelve-plus years, thrown away.

When we moved, my wife stopped most communication with her old friends. I never have. I am almost phobic about losing touch. I need to be in contact with people who knew me when I was better than I am now. It's one of the few ego strokes I still allow myself.

In my own crazed way, as I move forward as martyr for my married friends, I like to think my wife and I did them all a public service. That through all the shit I've dealt with, and continue to deal with, that somehow I'm a cautionary tale. In less sober moments, I've taken to reminding many of them to hug their spouses, to be as present as possible with them. Because the moment you stop, someone else is willing to step in, and that's the end of it all.

"When one person wants out, it's done."

ALIAS: Stacey

OCCUPATION: Designer

YEAR OF BIRTH: 1960

CURRENT MARRIAGE STATUS: Divorced

DO YOU HAVE ANY CHILDREN? Yes. Two—nineteen and fourteen years
old

YEAR OF MARRIAGE: 1986, 2004

HOW LONG YOU DATED BEFORE YOU WERE MARRIED: Five years,
six years

YEAR OF DIVORCE: Divorce 1: litigation/separation began 1996 and ended
2000; divorce 2: 2006

In my first marriage, I had Martha Stewart syndrome. Every time
my husband walked out the door for another business trip—every
two weeks, for two weeks—I altered the house late at night after
the kids were asleep. I painted the walls different colors several
times a year, rearranged and purchased new furniture, sewed cur-
tains, bedspreads, upholstered, reupholstered, just constantly and
obsessively seeking ways to alter the home and make it feel better.
I think I both aimed to paint a pretty picture and to throw him
off guard upon his return, like saying, "This is not your home."

When he was home, I entertained elaborately—handmak-
ing the invitations, creating some crazy theme for the table,
and cooking meals for up to thirty people in an effort to keep
busy and keep from being alone with him. I also had this small
garden that I tended to like a fanatic, trying to make as many
homegrown foods as possible for my children. With all the craziness in our marriage, I tried to super compensate by making
my mommy life extremely "normal" and stable. All the other
mommies were only half kidding when they joked that I had a
"hidden husband."

We met in college. He had a great sense of humor, was very adventurous, fun, exciting, and we had the same group of friends who did everything together. He may still be the only person on earth that shared my love of seeing Johnny Thunders perform. But I was not "in love" with him at any point. He pursued me very strongly, but the charm and persistence he used came to feel like a medieval torture device as the marriage went on.

He was paranoid, which I thought was part of his sense of humor. It was so profound that I really thought he was kidding. In college, he was convinced that this man was following him. I thought it was weird and quirky but I didn't really think he was Paranoid with a capital "P." As it turned out, he wasn't joking— he believes that he's always being followed and watched, and has made this paranoia real because government officials around the world do indeed keep tabs on him.

This will sound extremely crazy, but my kids were the hugest reason to end the marriage. When Bill Clinton was elected president and brought a dog to the White House, my son was given the homework assignment of writing to the president with a suggestion for naming this dog. My husband forbid him to do so, and told him that he was never, ever to contact anyone in the government because no one should be able to develop a file on him.

For years he kept telling me he was in the garment business with a few other things on the side. I started to question this after our second year of marriage when our bathroom sink broke and I phoned him. He told me the FBI was raiding his office, removing all the contents, and he couldn't really deal with the sink. The brown paper lunch bags filled with cash that paid for our existence, combined with this news flash, jolted me into wondering further. People in the clothing business have no reason to fear hidden microphones in their home.

As it turned out, much of his travel was related to dealing arms and pharmaceutical products. He kept ending up in countries that were in violent revolutions—the dates corresponded to incidents very clearly. He somehow managed to fly in just as all the airports were closed down. Often, he could be found burning papers in the fireplace or on the grill in the backyard.

Shocking is an understatement. There were so many secrets that were revealed as time went on it is really hard to determine who he was/is/will be. After years of meticulous sleuthing—breaking into his briefcase, his luggage, looking through his passport stamps, carefully listening to and asking questions of all these new friends—I uncovered that he was a criminal with blood on his hands and lots of money in his pockets. I'm talking about tens of thousands of dollars discovered several times literally in the laundry machine water. There were 3:00 A.M. phone calls from frantic men all over the world, which was very freaky, as they were pleading with me to tell them where my husband was. It was equally freaky to have no clue *where* he was.

But it wasn't until he began to pressure me to move to Hong Kong that I realized how much I did not want to be his wife. When I told him clearly and definitively that I did not want to go, he threatened me. He said, "Turn your back, or simply blink an eye, and I will make the kids disappear. You will never, ever be able to find them."

In the moment of his threats, I attained an intense resolve. He did bring out a strength that I did not know I possessed. Through all the alone time, I built up a life for myself and my children. I also do not scare easily and have a very healthy view of what constitutes a crisis versus a difficulty. All of my sleuthing skills served me well in preparing to calmly and intelligently dismember the marriage without my children disappearing.

In the end, my husband left the country. That divorce was a personal triumph after committing the stupidest mistake of my life.

* * *

Fairy tales convey different things as one ages. I once thought receiving flowers or jewelry from a lover was romantic, yet now I love to buy these things for girlfriends as a gesture of friendship. Romantic things now feel more powerful when it incorporates a little memory. If we had a great time on a beach, I would save a shell and present it months later, and would love receiving a similar gift. I think "romantic" ultimately switches away from "things" and into demonstrating appreciation for the bond you share.

Playing fairy godmother or white knight is a genuinely supportive aspect in marriage. When my partner is hurting, I want to wave a magic wand—that may be sexual, or gastronomic, visual, or poetic—but I want to make it all better. When I feel down, I want a white knight to do something heroic. No one can fix the problem for you, but a display of support is wonderful. When romance is used as seduction for an unwilling or uninterested partner, it does not work out well. In my first marriage, my husband would try to buy me jewelry or plan an awesome trip to seduce me. But it never felt genuine.

My second marriage was the complete opposite. We did not lie to each other. There were no shocking truths or events. It was safe, primarily focused on security. He was honest, morally strong, not adventurous. I was in love with him deeply.

We were together for six years, but the one year of being married changed everything. My business failing was the straw that broke his back. We faced financial pressure and could not survive the conflict because his sense of safety was so very threatened. I guess he felt as I did in my first marriage: endangered. I never thought it would end in divorce, which is always soul-shattering to both partners and their families. However, I do know that when one person wants out, it's done.

Cumulatively, I find myself feeling like a complete failure when it comes to marriage. But I would marry again. Both of my husbands called me "the rock" because I was capable, strong, and trusting. As backward as this may sound, I strive to become more *dependent* on a partner. I would like a "rock," too. I have not become more jaded, I do believe this is entirely realistic. Although I do meet many, many jaded people my age who find me to be very naive.

"This unbending companionship with her parents drove me bat-shit crazy."

ALIAS: Charles

OCCUPATION: Businessman

DATE OF BIRTH: 1944

CURRENT MARRIAGE STATUS: I married my second and current wife in
  1983

DO YOU HAVE ANY CHILDREN? Yes. Two sons (ages thirty-five and
  twenty-five) and one daughter (age thirty-two)

WHERE YOU GREW UP: Florida

WHERE YOU LIVE: DC

YEAR OF MARRIAGE: 1971, 1983

HOW LONG YOU DATED BEFORE YOU WERE MARRIED: Six months,
  one year

YEAR OF DIVORCE: 1980

My mother told me after the divorce that I was walking around with a ring in my pocket and I married the first girl who accepted. Was it love? I thought so at the time. But it ended on a very ugly note.

I recall during the first year of our marriage, she acknowledged that perhaps we'd made a mistake, and said that we should consider divorce. I talked her out of it. I was willing to persevere and attempt to make it work. One of the main problems was that she had never been away from home, and we were living fifteen hundred miles away from Mommy and Daddy. The daily phone calls, confiding in her mother, constantly asking her advice on minutiae . . . This unbending companionship with her parents drove me bat-shit crazy.

After I graduated from law school, we moved into a one-bedroom apartment in Washington, DC. When her parents came to visit, guess where they stayed? She would not allow them to stay in a hotel, which they could well afford. That always caused a huge fight. When we moved into a two-bedroom apartment and her family came to visit—all four of them, including her siblings—yep, they all stayed with us. All six of us shared one bathroom. It seemed like a house in Chinatown. When my parents came to visit, there was never any discussion. They did the right thing and always stayed in a hotel.

After several years of living in major cities across the country, we wound up moving to the same city as her parents, which proved to be the straw that broke the camel's back. Our marriage had been very fragile for many years and finally we visited a marriage counselor selected by my former spouse. She aggressively tried to pin the marital discord on me. But I made it clear to the counselor that one of our primary issues was that she had never cut the umbilical cord with her parents. She was more interested in their well-being than ours or our children's.

Finally, the counselor asked her where in the pecking order her parents and I stood. And to this day, I cannot forget her response.

"My parents are number one," she said. "And my husband is one-A."

When the counselor told her that she was wrong to have that attitude, my ex stormed out of the meeting. That evening, I told her the marriage was over and that I would file for divorce. We explained it to the children, and I moved out soon thereafter. Immediately following the divorce—and until her very recent remarriage—my ex has lived next door to her parents.

Before I got engaged, one of my married friends said to me, "Marriage is not just a bunch of dick and pussy." I thought it funny at the time, but if you really think about it, that has a lot of meaning.

A healthy marriage should include romance, passion, compatibility, and practicality. Of course, after several years the romance and passion is bound to become somewhat less frequent. After reaching age sixty, however, my wife and I can attest to the positive raves and FDA approval of Viagra and Cialis. Bless Pfizer. I'm just waiting for one of those four-hour hard-ons mentioned as a potential "risk" in the advertisements!

I do feel like I'm a lot wiser as a result of my first marriage. I learned to be aware of the in-laws. Although my current wife's mother was a difficult person at best, she knew how to handle her and was willing to stand up to her when necessary. She and I were raised in surprisingly similar manners, ranging from the food our mothers prepared to the prescribed medicines we took as children. It's no surprise that we share the same conservative political views and that her cousin is married to my cousin.

We make it a point to kiss each other good night and good morning every day, something I gleaned from my parents. Is it symbolic or a sign of affection? That is not even a question at this stage of my life.

"A good personality is just as important as a good sex life. You can learn how to be a good sexual partner."

ALIAS: Henrietta

OCCUPATION: Schoolteacher (retired)

YEAR OF BIRTH: 1931

CURRENT MARRIAGE STATUS: Divorced

DO YOU HAVE ANY CHILDREN? Two daughters

WHERE YOU GREW UP: Colorado

WHERE YOU LIVE: Colorado

YEAR OF MARRIAGE: 1953

HOW LONG YOU DATED BEFORE YOU WERE MARRIED: A year and
a half

YEAR OF DIVORCE: 1967

You got married over fifty-five years ago. Is there a piece of advice you can give me that is just as true now as it was then?
Be honest with each other. Be straightforward. Know each other's spending habits—you need to be on the same page about how to handle your finances. I think it's much more of a problem now than it was when I got married because all of us had grown up during the Depression when nobody had any money.

One of the men I interviewed said that the secret to marriage is not learning how to get along, but rather learning how to fight fairly and productively. How do you do that?
I didn't know anything about that when I was married, but there are techniques. Learning how to defuse the situation. Using "I" statements rather than "you" statements. Don't look to place blame. So instead of saying "you were this" or "you did that" say "this is what I feel and it makes me unhappy." But it takes a bit of insight into one's self to really be able to do that.

What did it mean to be "a good wife" in 1953?
At that time, the ideal was to be a stay-at-home wife and mother. His job was to go out and make the salary for us to live on and my job was to run the house and raise the children. I really had no choice. I did everything the *Ladies' Home Journal* said I should do. I was always well dressed—I don't think I ever came to breakfast in a bathrobe. My hair was always combed; I always had makeup on. And you always had the meals ready on time and you tried to be a good cook. My husband couldn't boil water [laughs]!

Did you enjoy any aspects of your "job"?
I liked raising the children; I didn't particularly like raising the house. Some people really do enjoy cooking. It took me fifty years to realize that I don't. So now I live in a retirement community where I don't cook, I don't shop, I don't do dishes. I get three meals a day prepared for me and it's an absolute joy. It's *wonderful.*

How did you meet your husband?
On a blind date in college. We were set up by one of my sorority sisters. He was a year older, I thought he was a pretty good-looking guy.

Did you fall hard for him?
It was gradual.

How did he propose?
We were sitting on the shore of Sloan's Lake in Denver and he asked me to marry him.

Did you have any doubt in your mind when you said "yes"?
No.

Did you live together before?
Oh, heavens, no! In 1953, that was not done. We were both students at the University of Colorado, so I was living in a sorority house and he was living in an apartment.

Did you have sex before you got married?
Yes.

Did a lot of girls do that?
It was happening but it was not out in the open. It was sub-rosa.

A girl could get a reputation?
Oh, yeah. She would get a reputation as being "easy" or "fast."

And then she'd be less desirable as a potential wife?
Right; she was *damaged goods*. I had several friends, sorority sisters, who ended up pregnant—and they got married very quickly [laughs]!

Did you have a lot in common with your husband? Were you compatible when it came to the day-to-day stuff?
Food, we were both pretty open. I was definitely a morning person and he was definitely a night person. I had been raised with a lot of classical music and he hadn't, but he grew to really like it. And we both shared interests in the sciences and we both liked to fish and hunt. I had been taught to fish and shoot by my father and had my own gun. In Colorado, there's a lot of good trout fishing. So we would go and do that together. That was something we enjoyed.

What did you hunt?
We hunted pheasants and ducks.

Were you the better shot?
I think we were about equal [laughs].

Did you have a healthy sex life with your husband?
In the beginning we did, but as he began to have more and more affairs it got sparser and sparser. We were both very naive because neither one of us had any previous sexual experience. But that was the way most people were back then.

Do you think it's better now that most people go into marriage with a fair amount of sexual experience?
I think it's much better, yeah. You get to find out if you're compatible in that way without going through all the hoopla. But I think a good personality is just as important as a good sex life. You can learn how to be a good sexual partner.

You mentioned your husband having affairs. Is that why you got divorced?
Well, after quite a while, he was drinking too much and I didn't like that. This was after ten years or so. And I didn't know it at the time but he was having a lot of affairs, yes.

How did you find out?
I had been a little bit suspicious and it was kind of a situation where: *Do I want to know or do I not want to know?* But then it just got to the point of: *I have to know.* So I did some detective work. Going through his wallet I saw some things that were a little strange. Because I had always been in charge of the family finances. I handled the budget, I paid all the bills, the investments, savings, everything. And then all of a sudden he decided to take all that over. Then he started going out after dinner for "a drive." And I would get calls from the phone company saying, "Will you accept the charges on a long-distance phone call?" And I said, "No, there's no reason to. Where are these calls coming from?" Well, the woman he was seeing was living in Texas. So I confronted him and he confessed that he had been having an affair with her. And after that, things fell apart.

211

Did you blame yourself?

Who else? I mean, I blamed myself to an extent. I certainly wasn't perfect. But I didn't know what I had done wrong. It was pretty awful. It left me with a real feeling of . . . a very poor sense of self-worth.

Were you open to reconciling after you found out, or was that a point of no return for you?

I think it was a point of no return because he had no desire to save the marriage.

Did he marry that woman?

The day after the divorce.

Have they been together ever since?

She died of throat cancer. He married again and died about ten years ago.

Did you go to his funeral?

No.

Did you hate him after you found out about the affair?

I tried not to hate him because I didn't want our daughters to hate him. So I tried to maintain a civil relationship for their sake. I didn't want to be the kind of a parent that was always talking against the other parent.

What's an example of something you learned the hard way?

I learned that I knew nothing about alcoholism. I knew nothing about Al-Anon or anything like that, so I was definitely an enabler.

How were you an enabler? Standing by and doing nothing?

Or by covering for him when he was hungover and couldn't go to work.

Do you remember the early warning signs? Any advice on how to spot them?

When you're going to a party and your partner wants to have a couple of drinks before going, that's not normal. And then when he's at the party, if he drinks too much and can't stop to the point where people say, "Take the keys away." And then if you're about to have a knockout fight to try and get the keys away. There were times when I was quite afraid for my own life because of his driving. Eventually I just stopped accepting invitations to parties because it turned out to be too much of a hassle.

How did he act when he was drunk?

He acted drunk [laughs]! He had no sense. I didn't like him when he was drunk. He wasn't ever mean to me. Well, there was verbal abuse but he never tried to hit me or anything like that. I was never a battered wife. He liked to put me down a lot verbally.

How would he put you down?

I remember there was one instance when he was going to France for the big Paris Air Show—he was working for Douglas Aircraft. And I expressed an interest in going because I had always wanted to go to France. And he said, "That would be like taking a sandwich to a banquet." It just hurt me horribly. There were a lot of remarks like that. When we finally broke up he said, "You'll have the children but I don't think you can handle it." And that really hurt. Because I handled it extremely well.

Were you ever able to say "It hurts my feelings when you say things like that"?

No, at the time, I wouldn't have said something like that. I wouldn't have tried to do things for my own pleasure.

It was a man's world?

Yeah, very much so. After our divorce, our daughters were taking piano lessons and I wanted to take piano lessons, too. And I thought, "Gee, I don't have to explain to anyone why I want to do that. Just because I want to is good enough!" When I was married, he would have said, "Why do you want to do that? What is that going to do?" And the fact that it would bring me personal pleasure wasn't a good enough reason, that wasn't acceptable.

Being a mother of two and divorced at thirty-six, did you feel like you were wearing a scarlet letter?
Not particularly. By the time I was divorced, in '67, that's when women's lib started up, and it had a very positive effect on my life because it gave me much more courage and support to go out and be a working mother and a single parent.

How else did the women's movement affect you?
My divorce happened just about the time *Ms.* magazine started. The first issue of that was published as part of *New York* magazine, which my brother had given me a subscription to, and I thought, "Oh, my God! They're describing my life!"

What were they writing about that was so revelatory for you?
That you can make it on your own, fight for your own rights. In fact, my elder daughter, going into eighth grade, she wanted to take woodshop, which was not open to girls. And I said, "I can't fight this for you, you have to go in yourself." And she managed to get in and she did fabulously well—and then they opened it to all the girls. This was all around '68 or '69, and to this day, my daughter enjoys doing fine woodwork.

Do you think gender roles have changed a lot since you got married?
Oh, yes. Very, very much. When I got married, most girls went to college to nab a husband. We did not go with the thought of a career path. We were programmed by society and by our parents

that it was a good place to find our life mate. And so that's what many of us did.

How did the Pill change your attitude toward sex?
Oh! Tremendously! It meant that you didn't always have that fear of getting pregnant. That and the IUD and the development of other kinds of birth control. Just *tremendous*. All of a sudden it was all out in the open. I think back to my grandmother's era, when you didn't talk about sex at all. I mean, here she is, she has six children and you weren't ever supposed to talk about how they got there! You weren't ever supposed to enjoy it! The Pill enabled us to enjoy sex, which most of us didn't know how to do.

Do you think gender relations just keep getting better?
If we define "better" as the genders having more freedom to pursue their own lives, then yes, I think that's healthy. I think that makes for happier people.

Is there anything that we've lost? Something that was better in your day?
I think maybe we've lost a lot of common courtesy. Kindness. Being polite to each other. What people might now consider to be a more old-fashioned way of living. That had a lot going for it, too.

**"Ninety percent of the secret to being married is the commitment to the
process of being married. Whatever comes your way—problems with
sex, problems with money, whatever—it's essential that you're both
committed to working out a solution where both people are represented,
where the well-being of the other person is just as—if not *more*—important than your own."**

ALIAS: Ruby

OCCUPATION: Real estate

YEAR OF BIRTH: 1976

CURRENT MARRIAGE STATUS: Divorced

DO YOU HAVE ANY CHILDREN? Nope

WHERE YOU GREW UP: Alabama

WHERE YOU LIVE: New York

YEAR OF MARRIAGE: 1999

HOW LONG YOU DATED BEFORE YOU WERE MARRIED: Four years

YEAR OF DIVORCE: 2009

My father always said, "Don't get married until you're thirty.
You don't know what you're doing until you're thirty." My parents met at twenty-one and got married a year later. That didn't
work out; they got divorced when I was seven. So my father just
sort of figured that you have no concept of who you are and what
you want until you turn thirty.

Seth and I met when I was nineteen and he was twenty. I
believe it was in a German theology class. Nothing turns me on
like a man with a really thick brain, and I thought he was one of
the smartest people I'd ever met. We didn't get together in college, but we were friendly. After college, he was at Columbia
for grad school and I was at NYU and we started hanging out. I
remember having Chinese food on his roof one night and it just
suddenly felt magical. It was like walking into a movie and here

was my happy ending—here was my "happily ever after." As far as my twenty-one-year-old self could tell, I had been struck by an arrow of Cupid. It was overwhelming.

I felt a real sense of certainty and connection to him. And I was one of these people who was like, "I will not make the mistakes that my parents made—I understand that being married is hard work and requires focus and determination." In fact, I was so hypervigilant that when we first started talking about marriage, I made us go to a therapist. Couples counseling before we even got *engaged*. I wanted to make sure that we would never get divorced, no matter what. I was going to *guarantee* it.

Of course, hindsight's 20/20, so now I can see all the issues that we had. I'm trying to think of a nonjudgmental way to say this . . . I'm not a person with a lot of boundaries; I'm very interested in emotional intimacy and messiness. I like close quarters in that regard. I'm one of five kids, and I like a lot of engagement with family and friends and community. So while at first Seth found that charming, I think ultimately he started to find it overwhelming. He is somebody with a *lot* of boundaries. He just really likes to be by himself. He has, like, two close friends. I mean, this is a stupid example, but on Facebook, I had like eight hundred friends and he had twenty-three. On Flickr, he's the guy who has photographs of his cat and his new bed. That's what he's sharing with the world.

So during our marriage, when we were invited places, I would always go by myself. I just figured, "Okay, different strokes for different folks. It's not his thing, I'm not going to force him." I had made the mistake of trying to make him go to things when he didn't want to, and that didn't make *anybody* happy. He was miserable the whole time and then I couldn't enjoy myself because I was so focused on how unhappy he was.

I do think Seth loved me so much and for so long that he really did try to change who he was—to go from somebody who was essentially introverted and isolated to somebody who was extroverted and engaged. But when it came down to having kids, he just couldn't push past that boundary.

When we turned thirty—or when *I* turned thirty—I started to get really obsessive about the kid thing. It was like, "Okay, maybe not *now,* but when in the next two years are we going to try to get pregnant?" To his credit, he was very clear about all this. He kept saying, "I really don't know if I *want* to have kids." And I was like, "Of *course* you want to have kids! Who doesn't want to have kids?" I really just refused to hear him. And I guess that's what ultimately broke us up.

I think there's this popular misconception about sex in a marriage: that you get bored, or that it's the same type of thing over and over again. And that can set in, sure. But when things were good between us, the fact that we were married actually made things *more* intense. Because you're so completely at ease with the other person, you know you're so loved by them, and that can be amazing. But sex is the ultimate form of communication, and when that communication breaks down it becomes very hard to want the other person in any serious way. And because I wanted a child so badly, sex became loaded in that regard. The first year we were together, Seth and I must've had sex five or six times a week. By the last year of our marriage, we maybe had sex five or six times that year.

I suppose in some weird, judgmental way, I always thought that affairs were symptoms of moral character. And now I see them for what they are. It is a crying out of feeling totally alone within your own marriage—sexual isolation or emotional isolation—which is the scariest feeling because there's no recourse. When you're single, there's a possibility that you're going to fall in love. You might be lonely, but you dwell in that type of possibility. When you're married and things are shitty there's nowhere to go. So you really start to resent the person. And there were moments when things got really bad between Seth and me. I remember looking at each other and both probably thinking, "You are the place that my hope has gone to die."

One time, I was sitting with him in his study—he has a PhD in theology—and he was reading me some article. And I just remember thinking to myself, "I'm never going to give a shit about this. I can fake it for a while, but I'm never *really* going to care." So it was unfair for me to have to listen to it and it was incredibly unfair for him to have a partner who couldn't sustain some sort of interest in his work. But when the fact that I wasn't interested enough became a point of recrimination, it wasn't one of those things where he could just accept it and be like, "All right, she gives me this and this, but not this and this." Instead, I would get accusations that I wasn't intellectual enough. I remember being in bed and him touching me and me thinking, "You've gotta be fucking kidding me. All you do is make me feel like shit and then you want to get *laid*? What, are you crazy?"

So we got into our own little vicious cycle. The more I needed him, the more withdrawn he became, and the more susceptible I became to the attention of other men. I had what I call a number of "emotional affairs," which were very serious, involved friendships that felt emotionally like love affairs even if, physically, I only kissed one person once. This somehow seemed okay in my mind even though I knew that if I had found out that he was doing this I would've been devastated. Behind all of this, I think, was an incredible desire to *provoke* Seth. I didn't want my marriage to end; I wanted him to wake up and be present.

At one point I was pretty convinced that I was in love with one of these other guys. I had gone to a conference and this person had been there and I ended up sleeping with him in the same bed, spooning, lying in his arms all night. It got really, really close, but nothing had transpired. I had written all about it in my journal and left it out. I mean, it's so obvious I wanted to get caught. And of course Seth ended up reading it, which led to a complete blowout.

I have a very clear image of him coming into my room, looking at me with this absolute shock on his face, and it cutting me in my gut. I felt like I'd gotten kicked and that I deserved it. I don't mean that I deserved to be kicked—I mean that I deserved to be kicked *multiple* times. But of course my response was, "Why did you read that?!"

My stepmom had all these great lines about marriage that I thought were completely ludicrous when I first heard them, but the longer I was married, I felt they were really right-on. One was, "You can be right or you can be married." Or, "Marriage isn't a 50/50 compromise—it's a *100* percent compromise. Neither person totally gets what they want."

I'm sorry if that sounds cynical, but people who think that *love conquers all,* I just wonder if they've ever been married. Ninety percent of the secret to being married is the commitment to the *process* of being married. Whatever comes your way—problems with sex, problems with money, whatever—it's essential that you're both committed to working out a solution where both people are represented, where the well-being of the other person is just as—if not *more*—important than your own. It's an easy thing to say ideologically, but it's really, really hard to do, especially the younger you are.

Look, if you're willing to suck it up, you can make just about anything work, but it takes two to carry it. The question is, do you come to a point where you compromise yourself into oblivion, where you just cease to exist? I think that is the real danger about staying in a bad relationship. And I remember definitely thinking that. Like if I had just given up on the child thing and it was okay to go everywhere by myself and essentially be isolated within my own marriage, I'd probably still be married. If I had tried a little harder, if I had done a little better, if I had not been so demanding, if I had been more understanding, maybe it could have worked. I think part of me is still haunted by that idea. And there are people who do make those choices. But I just think I would've woken up at forty, homicidal and ready to kill him. We would've been one of those couples who were married for fifty years and hated the sight of each other.

Emotionally, it's just devastating to suddenly be single, especially if you've been married your whole adult life. It's *shocking*. It's like this seismic shift that people don't warn you about. In popular culture, it's depicted as this great liberation, but it sure as hell doesn't feel that way.

When you're married, your frame of reference for a relationship is, you know, let's go to Target, we'll run some errands, clean up the garage, then maybe in the afternoon we'll take a nap and have sex, and then we're seeing the so-and-sos for dinner. You know that there's no hiding your complexity from the other person or the other person hiding their complexity from you. Eventually all your shit comes out and it comes out in full force, so you might as well stop pretending sooner rather than later.

When you're dating, it feels like you're involved in this elaborate public relations event where, as Chris Rock says, the ambassador of you is meeting the ambassador of them, and suddenly you're getting dressed up and receiving a beautiful bouquet of flowers, getting taken out for a three-hundred-dollar dinner, and having a bottle of wine on a Thursday night. And you're just like, "What the hell is this?" You feel like Alice in Wonderland. It's not that it's not *fun*; it's just not *real*. It's substanceless. Personally, I prefer Target.

EPILOGUE

I'd been Googling again. It always picks up around the dog days of August because I was born on September 1, and birthdays tend to send me into the ether, looking for answers. One night, late, after an extensive, cross-referential search, I figured out what the following men have in common: da Vinci, Aquinas, van Gogh, Newton, Kant, Thoreau, George Gershwin, Nietzsche, Vivaldi, Chopin, Toulouse-Lautrec, Handel, Schubert, Copernicus, Beethoven, and Voltaire.

Were they geniuses in their respective fields? Sure. But they were also lifelong bachelors. I realize, of course, that I'm not in their company, brainwise. And that many of them weren't necessarily "marriage material"—some were gay and others were pretty irascible, if not psychotic. Still, I began to feel a kinship with their lowly relationship status, as if maybe it was meant to be mine.

Maybe these divorce interviews were getting to me after all.

Earlier in the day, my housemate's girlfriend came over and hung a variety of "Welcome Home!" banners as a surprise. It wasn't their anniversary or his birthday or anything, she just felt like doing it because he'd been away on a trip and she missed him. As I watched her find the perfect spots on the walls, I realized: I want to be the one hanging the banners.

Why have I never hung banners?

I asked my friend Lisa over dinner that night and she said, "No one's ever knocked your socks off."

"Not true," I said. "I've had my socks knocked off plenty of times. *Five* times. Six, if you count that thing with the girl from Nashville."

"Right, but it always ends the same way."

"What way?"

"You get cold feet."

She's right.

**What happens is, the utter grandeur and magnificence
of what love actually is gets overshadowed by this disappointment
that it's not the way we fantasized it should be.**

Everything changed on August 28, 2011, when I met a crystal-wearing girl from Costa Rica named Ashley. I'm not too crazy about the whole crystal thing. They're cool-looking, I guess, but I don't buy into all that stuff about how waxing moons and rising tides affect the ions of a rock, and how that "healing energy" can somehow balance the chakras in our bodies. Truth be told, I don't really know what chakras are, and I don't usually fall for girls who do. But this book has taught me that when it comes to love, the word "usually" means nothing.

Ashley is a twenty-nine-year-old, Mexican Canadian, yoga-bodied vegetarian who makes pesto with local cashews because pine nuts come from Spain and she won't eat anything that wasn't grown within a hundred miles of her kitchen. The crystal that she wore—egg-shaped and made of jade—wasn't hanging from a decorative string around her neck, or her wrist, or kept in her pocket for good luck or good vibes. She told me all about its power, purpose, and position while we were lying in bed, six hours after we met. I paused and then responded, "Without question, 'I have a jade crystal in my cervix' is the most original thing I've ever heard on a first date."

Granted, this wasn't your average first date. It began somewhat spontaneously, lasted more than ten hours without a split second of awkwardness, and we haven't seen each other since, unless you count the three-hundred-plus hours of "dating" we've done on Skype.

(Ridiculous, I know.)

We met the day she passed through Venice without a driver's license or a credit card, on her way to a dream analysis workshop in Santa Barbara with her grandmother. She carried a sack of homegrown fruit—mangosteen, jackfruit, sapodilla—and I'm pretty sure she had the same cell phone that Gordon Gekko used on the beach in *Wall Street* (somehow it could text). She was wearing a sexy-skimpy tank top and what I assumed was a skirt but later realized were a pair of drop-crotch genie pants that MC Hammer and Krusty the Clown might have fought over in the early '90s. Forty-five minutes after we met, I looked down at her ankles and thought, "Wait, are those *pants*?"

Still, I couldn't stop staring at her. She had a nose ring and an accent and she seemed to take great pleasure in feeding me jagged squares of dark chocolate made from criollo cacao beans that were harvested, fermented, and roasted on the permaculture farm where she lives in the jungle near Puerto Viejo. By the way, don't feel like you've been living in a Wal-Mart if you haven't heard of half these words. Three months ago, neither had I.

Opposites attract, it's a simple fact.

Ashley is a teacher at a Waldorf-inspired kindergarten in the Talamanca region of Costa Rica. In addition to showing the children how to become freethinking, morally responsible individuals, she tells them how to make nice with local monkeys, sloths, toucans, and iguanas, and how to steer clear of the eyelash pit viper, poisonous dart frogs, bullet ants, scorpions, tarantulas, and prickly plants such as the stinging nettle and the spiny zarzaparrilla root. In class, they make tea tree mouthwash and cinnamon-coconut toothpaste, but there are no modern toys of any kind: no screens, no plastic, nothing that runs on batteries.

During "imaginative playtime" they draw with natural beeswax crayons and act out fantastical scenarios using faceless rag dolls and organically shaped blocks of wood.

It's worth noting here that I prefer Damon Runyon to Rudyard Kipling, and that for three summers in a row I slept under a mosquito net with a view of the Gowanus Canal. (For those of you who don't know, the Gowanus is a foul-smelling body of still water—in Brooklyn.) I was raised on microwaves, Toucan Sam, Dig 'Em the Frog, and if I'm on a road trip, I actually look forward to getting a Spicy Chicken Sandwich and a Frosty from Wendy's. I put real gas in my car, I've never been to a healer or a guru, and I tend to cringe a bit when someone starts or ends a sentence with "holistically speaking." Did I say "cringe"? I fucking hate that phrase. Ashley hates it, too, but she would never say "fucking." She rarely swears. I swear all the time.

Temperament is important; temperature is not.

We met because of an e-mail. Our mutual friend Stephen, a fruit farmer who has lived in the Caribbean since 1995, sent us a note urging us to connect. "I want you guys to meet!!!" he wrote. And then again, later: "Just make sure you guys meet!!!" So we made plans for three o'clock at the coffee shop where I go every morning, which I no longer think of as *the coffee shop where I go every morning* but rather *the place I first saw Ashley's face*.

Our first interaction via text (which I still have) was on August 28, 2011, at 2:59 P.M.—and it went like this:

Me: "I am here. Wave your arms."
Ashley: "Peeing."

I'm not sure why, but I thought that this was the most auspicious opening exchange of all time. A minute later she emerged from the bathroom and all I could think was:

It's *you.*

That's what it felt like. Like being in a movie. Heart-stopping, slow-motion, with a swelling score. Then silence as I went to shake her hand and she gave me this "don't be silly" look, hugged me, and planted a real kiss on my cheek. It was the first time I'd ever truly contemplated the possibility of past lives. How else to explain this seemingly cosmic instant connection? Instant attraction is one thing: It's visceral, chemical, pheromonal. But when all those things combine with a genuine familiarity in broad daylight and without any alcohol, it really makes you wonder.

Is it you?

I played it cool because you have to play it cool in these situations; otherwise you look like a lunatic, asking a stranger where they've been all your life—let alone all your past lives. So I bought her a coffee and we walked into a bookstore where for some reason I picked up a paperback called *1001 Questions to Ask Before You Get Married.* We sat down at a table by the window and she smiled at me with a disarming complicity. I opened the book, ready to fire away, but we didn't get to a single question because we just couldn't stop talking. It wasn't your typical get-to-know-you chitchat—it was almost as if we were catching up, reminiscing, skimming through decades, maybe even centuries, to arrive at this very moment in time.

Is it really *you?*

Ten hours later, after staying up all night, she was gone.

Passion? I know it's overrated.
That adrenaline rush, it's not real.

Today is December 9, 2011. It's been 102 days since we met at the coffee shop, and since then, twelve hours haven't passed without us speaking, chatting, e-mailing, texting, or Skyping. "How's your fantasy girlfriend?" my friends ask. I've stopped trying to explain it because, frankly, it makes me a little uneasy to hear the words coming out of my mouth. Scanning the pages of our chat transcripts, it's actually rather embarrassing—rational adults routinely sending *X*s and *O*s and emoticons, staring into our cameras for hours, eating together, reading together, falling asleep together, and saying things like:

> Me: Hang up.
> Ashley: You.
> Me: I hung up last night.
> Ashley: Walk away, I can't do it if I see your face.

Every night at the end of our video sessions we do this thing where we just kind of stare at each other for a while, without speaking. Ashley calls it a "wind-down." One time, I broke the moment by typing, "You look more and more familiar to me." It turned into this big discussion about visions and hallucinations—how the heart is *gullible* above all things—and whether this "love" of ours is genuine and sustainable. We talked about the sheer craziness of it all, how we're living on a cloud, and how clouds are vaporous and ephemeral. We both fully acknowledged that we've spent just ten hours in each other's actual presence and that this head-over-heels euphoria, as authentic as it feels, is equal parts illusion, delusion, projection, and fantasy.

Still, we gaze.

A few weeks ago she texted me, "I put too much salt in the soup today. You know what that means, right?"

"What?" I wrote.

"It means I'm in love!"

And to be honest, my first thought was, "Is it *me*?"

It's not a question of winning love from people.
It's either there or it isn't—there's nothing you can do
other than be yourself.

Ashley is flying in from Costa Rica tomorrow, December 10. She's staying with me for three weeks. We'll celebrate her birthday, Chanukah, Christmas, New Year's—"and winter solstice," she adds. Is this lust? Sure. Infatuation? Certainly. Is it love? I have no idea. Only time will tell. But like my grandma, I now keep company with spirits—the voices in this book—and I'm both haunted and guided by their wisdom.

So from now on, I'm going to do my best to accelerate the inevitable, discuss the dirty, and engage the elephants. To hold on loosely. To not overly prioritize the eternal. I won't paint the red flags white. I'm going to fall freely, truthfully, without fear, and without socks. I'm going to eliminate the *ish* and just admit my shit. No rules, no games. There's just no other way to do it.

If I end up being alone, so be it.
But I don't want to fake anything ever, ever, ever again.

Now, if you'll excuse me, I have banners to hang.

THE QUESTIONNAIRE

---

1. What percentage of your friends have gotten divorced? What percentage of your married friends would say they are happy with their relationship?

2. Opposites may attract, but do they remain attracted? Discuss the importance of having things in common: the food you like to eat, the shows you like to watch, the times you wake up and go to sleep. Please give specific examples.

3. What did you love about your spouse? Did they change after you got married? How so? Is there always some level of idealizing and fantasy in the beginning of a relationship?

4. What about the little things? The hair in the drain, leaving the toilet seat up . . . any specific peccadilloes you can recall? And is it ever *really* about the peccadilloes—or do we just use these things to get at the bigger issues?

5. Talk about compromise. Discuss the difference between *fusing* and *losing* your identity. Did you feel "completed" or "crowded" in your marriage? Did your sense of self blossom or wither? Did your spouse bring out the best in you? Please give specific examples.

6. Is it true that in a relationship there is always an inequality between the lover and the loved? Which one were you? Did it change over time?

7. How did your parents' marriage (or divorce) affect you? Were they role models, or just the opposite? Please talk about specific memories that shaped your view.

8. How important is total honesty in a marriage? When—if ever—is it okay to lie? What were some lies that you told—and why? What were some lies that were told to you?

9. Were there any shocking truths that you uncovered during the marriage or after the separation? What were they? How did you discover them, and what impact did they have? When does a lie become unforgivable?

10. Some say the key to a good marriage is diminished expectations. Do you agree? Is a healthy marriage more about passion and romance or compatibility and practicality?

11. Define romance. Is there a danger in being *too* romantic, believing in fairy tales?

12. Who is more "romantic"—men or women? Does this change over the course of a marriage? Does the definition of "romantic" change?

13. Was there any kind of "big incident" you can point to as the cause of your breakup? If there was an incident (infidelity, for example), please explain what happened in as much detail as possible.

14. Was it a mutual decision to end your marriage?

15. Looking back, do you think that deep down you always knew it would end? That you were just wrong for each other? If so, what were some of the early warning signs?

16. Rank the following stresses in your relationship: sex, conversation, money, in-laws. Please give examples.

17. How important is sex? How did your sex life change over the course of your marriage? Did it get better or worse? Was there tension over who initiated sex more? Jealousy? Unexplored fantasies? Lack of spontaneity or variety? Any advice on how to keep the sparks flying?

18. How many sexual partners did you have before getting married? Do you wish you had more or less? What impact, if any, does this type of experience (or lack thereof) have on a marriage?

19. There is a quote, "The chain of wedlock is so heavy that it takes two to carry it—sometimes three." What does this mean to you? Is monogamy more of a choice or a sacrifice? What is it about cheating that hurts so much? Is it a rational pain or more of an ego bruise?

20. Men are much more likely to pay for sex. Women are more likely to have an emotional affair. Why is that? If you cheated—or were cheated on—what's the difference between paid-for sex and an affair? Is one type of betrayal somehow "better" than the other?

21. Can adultery in the head be as destructive as adultery in the bed? Is there a "good" kind of jealousy and a "bad" kind of jealousy? Please give examples.

22. How has the Internet affected relationships? Facebook, dating sites, texting, porn? Is it easier to carry on an affair these days? Is it easier to get caught? Is it easier to walk away from a relationship because of all the new ways to meet people?

23. Did any form of addiction play a role in your divorce: drugs, alcohol, gambling, sex? Any form of abuse: physical or emotional?

24. If you had children, were they more of a bond or a wedge in your relationship? Were you more open to "working it out" because of them? Can you ever really stay together for the kids?

25. Do you believe in fate or destiny—that there is one "right" person for everyone? Has this view changed from when you were a child?

26. Are you jaded now? Less trusting? Wiser? More self-reliant?

27. Before you got married, were you the type to say, "I would never get divorced"? Do you think less of yourself because of the divorce? Do you consider it a personal failure? A triumph?

28. Why did you get married? Was it for love? If you could go back in time, would you do it all over again? Or do you regret it?

29. Would you marry again? If so, what would have to be different?

30. If you had to give one bit of advice to a friend who is about to get married, what would it be?

ACKNOWLEDGMENTS

"When you've got so much to say,
it's called gratitude."
—The Beastie Boys

Acknowledgments are all about naming names, of course, but in this case the boldest of the bunch will go unrecognized. To the anonymous donors who shared their stories, I'm forever grateful that you let me stand on your shoulders. Daniel Greenberg, my agent; Nan Graham, Whitney Frick, and everyone at Scribner—thank you for seeing a spark where others saw doom and gloom. Stephanie Lee, this would be a pile of tapes without you—thank you for all your tireless work and for your nine-grain'd wisdom. Alix Taylor and Daisy Lee, I'd have lost ten pounds while writing were it not for you; thank you for always being there with a hot meal, a hot lead, and the latest from Nicki Minaj. Danielle Birrittella, the girl from up the street—I'm so happy that you moved across the country and around the corner. Thank you for seeing me to the finish line. And to my friends and colleagues who helped out in ways too numerous to mention: Carra Greenberg, Evan Wiener, Michelle Kroes, Adam Sack, Jeff Mandel, Randy Manis, Sarah Treem, Chris Norris, Casey McIntyre, Stacey Reiss, Lindsay Marcus, Nick Karno, Greg Stern, Michael Spiccia, Alan Light, Lou Cove, Dave Getson, Adam Kulakow, Streeter Phillips, Sylvie Rabineau, Brian Young, Liz Biber, Tara Summers, Lorien Haynes, Stacey Kalish, Sara Wilson, Jenny

Jue, Sarah Adler, Hayley Starr, Todd Krieger, Andrew Hurwitz, Geoff Sanford, Roger Bennett, Richard Anthony Blake, Aleksandra Evanguelidi, Jeremy Kotin, Sara Bernstein, Neil Feineman, David Melamed, Daryl Roth, Scott and Johanna Lasky, Frally Hynes, Stephen Brooks, Marjorie Shapiro, Scott Minkow, Alison Busch, Tim Perrell, Elisa Pugliese, Mark Zupan, Jason and Sylvana Krasner, David and Dara Rosenberg, Robin Dolch, Sivan Baron, Gina Kapustin, Ben Schuman, Dean Tye, Lisa Danna, Lisa Newman Levine, Rachel Rouffe, Jennifer Kosow, Paul Galicia, Evan Bienstock, Jen Sall, Stuart Banerjee, Sharon Shane, Leslie Zises, Corey Scholibo, Cynthia Vanis, Lowell Sears, MJ Lee, Celine Coudert, Dawn Wechsler, Adam Sternbergh, Karen Chmielnicki, Sylvia Becker, Uncle Saul, Uncle Ralph, Aunt Evie, Jay Feather, Abigail Ulman, Lara Meyerratken, Bolaji Akran, Fred Kramer, Michaela Watkins, Jennifer Almadoce, Dash Boyer-Olson, Jonathan Rouffe, Sean McLean, Larry Honig, Lauren Schwartz, Jessica Edwards, Dan Berger, David Fenkel, and everyone at Oscilloscope—especially Adam Yauch: May he pass the mic and rest in peace. To the man who sang torch songs while doing his laundry, I could always hear you from my desk in the garage. You're a rock star. To Ashley, for always showing me new worlds. And finally, firstly, to my family: Mom, Dad, Mimi, Rachel, John, Hannah, Jordan, Abby, and Griff—I love you very much and I thank you for always standing behind me and walking beside me at the same time.